THE TIMES TOP 100 GRADUATE EMPLOYERS

The definitive guide to the leading employers
recruiting graduates during 2006-2007.

HIGH FLIERS

**HIGH FLIERS PUBLICATIONS LTD
IN ASSOCIATION WITH THE TIMES**

Published by High Fliers Publications Limited
10a Belmont Street, Camden Town, London NW1 8HH
Telephone: **020 7428 9100**   Web: **www.Top100GraduateEmployers.com**

Editor **Martin Birchall**
Publisher **Gill Thomas**
Production Manager **Robin Burrows**
Portrait Photography **Robert Hollingworth** www.roberthollingworth.co.uk

The Times Top 100 Graduate Employers is based on research results
from *The UK Graduate Careers Survey 2006,* produced by High Fliers
Research Ltd.

The greatest care has been taken in compiling this book. However, no
responsibility can be accepted by the publishers or compilers for the
accuracy of the information presented.

Where opinion is expressed it is that of the author or advertiser and
does not necessarily coincide with the editorial views of High Fliers
Publications Limited or The Times newspaper.

Printed and bound in Great Britain by CPI Bath Press.

A CIP catalogue record for this book
is available from the British Library.
ISBN 09536991-7-X or 97809536991-7-9

Contents

	Page
Foreword	5
Compiling the Top 100 Graduate Employers	9
Understanding the Graduate Market	19
Successful Job Hunting	29

Employer Entries

	Page		Page		Page
Accenture	40	Dstl	98	Mercer HR Consulting	150
Addleshaw Goddard	42	Ernst & Young	100	Merrill Lynch	152
Airbus	44	Eversheds	102	Metropolitan Police	154
Aldi	46	ExxonMobil	104	Microsoft	156
Allen & Overy	48	Financial Services		Ministry of Defence	158
Arcadia	50	Authority	106	Morgan Stanley	160
Army	52	Freshfields Bruckhaus		Nationwide	162
ASDA	54	Deringer	108	NGDP for	
AstraZeneca	56	Fujitsu	110	Local Government	164
Atkins	58	GCHQ	112	NHS	166
BAE Systems	60	GlaxoSmithKline	114	Oxfam	168
Baker & McKenzie	62	Goldman Sachs	116	Police - High Potential	
Barclays Bank	64	Google	118	Development Scheme	170
Barclays Capital	66	Grant Thornton	120	PricewaterhouseCoopers	172
BBC	68	HBOS	122	Procter & Gamble	174
Bloomberg	70	HSBC	124	QinetiQ	176
BP	72	IBM	126	Reuters	178
BT	74	John Lewis	128	Rolls-Royce	180
Cadbury Schweppes	76	JPMorgan	130	Royal Bank of	
Cancer Research UK	78	KPMG	132	Scotland Group	182
Citigroup	80	L'Oréal	134	Sainsbury's	184
Civil Service Fast Stream	82	Linklaters	136	Shell	186
Clifford Chance	84	Lloyds TSB	138	Slaughter and May	188
Corus	86	Lovells	140	Teach First	190
Credit Suisse	88	Marks & Spencer	142	Tesco	192
Data Connection	90	Mars	144	UBS	194
Deloitte	92	McDonald's Restaurants	146	Unilever	196
Deutsche Bank	94	McKinsey & Company	148	WPP	198
DLA Piper	96				

Information Request Service   200

Find out more about Britain's top employers and you could win an iPod Nano or start your career £5,000 richer!

Foreword

by Martin Birchall
Editor, The Times Top 100 Graduate Employers

Welcome to the latest edition of *The Times Top 100 Graduate Employers*, your guide to the UK's leading employers who are recruiting graduates in 2006-2007. If you're one of the quarter of a million final year university students due to graduate in the summer of 2007, then the employment outlook is very encouraging. The employers featured in the *Top 100* hired record numbers of graduates in 2005-2006 and are set to recruit even larger numbers this year.

There are currently more than 500 major employers in the UK who operate a recognised graduate recruitment scheme and promote their vacancies to university students. In addition, there are literally hundreds of small and medium-sized businesses that also recruit graduates into their organisations, often from local universities. This means that up to 200 different recruiters are expected to hold recruitment events or take part in campus careers fairs at many of the universities most popular with employers.

With such a wide choice of different types of employment and graduate jobs, how can prospective employers be assessed and ranked?

To find out, we interviewed over 16,000 final year students who graduated from universities across the UK in the summer of 2006, and asked them "Which employer do you think offers the best opportunities for graduates?" Between them, the 'Class of 2006' named organisations from every imaginable employment sector and business type – from major manufacturers to the 'Big Four' accounting & professional services firms, government departments to investment banks, leading charities to well-known IT companies and consulting firms. The one hundred employers who were mentioned most often during the research form *The Times Top 100 Graduate Employers*.

This book is therefore a celebration of the employers who are judged to offer the brightest prospects for graduates. Whether by the quality of their training programmes, the business success that they enjoy, the scale of their organisations, or by the impression that their recruitment promotions have made – these are the employers that are most attractive to university-leavers in 2006.

The Times Top 100 Graduate Employers book will not necessarily identify which organisation is right for you: only you can decide that. But it is an invaluable reference if you want to discover which graduate jobs Britain's leading employers offer. Leaving university and finding your first job can be a daunting process but it is one of the most important steps you'll ever take. Having a good understanding of the range of opportunities available must be the best way to start.

Martin Birchall writes a weekly Top 100 column for 'Career', the jobs & employment section of The Times.

Graduate opportunities, all disciplines.

If you want a career that offers more of the things that really count, welcome to AstraZeneca. We turn good ideas into effective medicines and our innovation enhances the lives of patients around the world.

If you're a graduate with serious talent and big ambitions, you'll never be just another face in the crowd. Our approach to development is focused on giving you the support you need to reach your potential – and rewarding your performance as an individual.

I want
to be
recognised

Find the recognition you deserve at
ideas.astrazeneca.com
sign up for job alerts and let the opportunities come to you

AstraZeneca
life inspiring ideas

Compiling the Top 100 Graduate Employers

by Gill Thomas
Publisher, High Fliers Publications Ltd

This year's university finalists and recent graduates hoping to start a first job in 2007 should certainly have an excellent choice of prospective employers. Job vacancies for new graduates have increased steadily for the last four years and there are expected to be over five thousand organisations competing to hire the best graduates from UK universities during the 2006-2007 recruitment season.

This huge choice can make selecting the employer that is 'right' for you much more difficult. How should you evaluate all the different opportunities and what determines which employers offer the best graduate positions? What are the main criteria that you can use to assess so many organisations and jobs?

These questions have no simple answers and clearly no one individual employer can ever hope to be right for every graduate – everyone makes their own judgements about the organisations they want to work for and the type of job they find the most attractive.

How then can anyone produce a meaningful league table of Britain's leading graduate employers? What criteria can define whether one organisation is 'better' than another? To compile *The Times Top 100 Graduate Employers*, the independent market research company, High Fliers Research Ltd, interviewed 16,452 final year students who left UK universities in the summer of 2006. The students from the 'Class of 2006'

who took part in the study were selected at random to represent the full cross-section of finalists at their universities, not just those who had already secured graduate employment. The research examined students experiences during their search for a graduate job and asked them about their attitudes to employers.

The key question used to produce the *Top 100* was "Which employer do you think offers the best opportunities for graduates?" This question was deliberately open-ended and students were not prompted in any way. Across the whole survey, finalists mentioned more than 500 different organisations – from the smallest local employers, to some of the world's best-known companies. The responses were analysed to identify the number of times each employer was mentioned. The one hundred organisations that were mentioned most often are the *The Times Top 100 Graduate Employers* for 2006.

The considerable selection of answers given by finalists from the 'Class of 2006' show that individual students used very different criteria to determine which employer they considered offered the best opportunities for graduates. Some focused on employers' general reputations – their public image, their business profile or their commercial success. Others evaluated employers based on the information they had seen during their job search – the quality of recruitment promotions, the impression formed

THE TIMES

TOP 100

GRADUATE EMPLOYERS

The Top 100 Graduate Employers 2006

This Year	Last Year		This Year	Last Year	
1.	1	PricewaterhouseCoopers	51.	51	Arcadia Group
2.	6	Deloitte	52.	36	ASDA
3.	4	KPMG	53.	85	Google
4.	2	Civil Service	54.	41	Foreign Office
5.	5	BBC	55.	44	Eversheds
6.	7	NHS	56.	50	Merrill Lynch
7.	8	HSBC	57.	59	Freshfields Bruckhaus Deringer
8.	3	Accenture	58.	39	Arup
9.	10	Procter & Gamble	59.	66	Atkins
10.	9	Goldman Sachs	60.	86	Data Connection
11.	12	Shell	61.	63	HBOS
12.	22	Aldi	62.	75	WPP
13.	11	Army	63.	61	ExxonMobil
14.	14	Ernst & Young	64.	71	Lovells
15.	15	Royal Bank of Scotland Group	65.	78	Bain & Company
16.	19	Teach First	66.	74	Cancer Research
17.	13	GlaxoSmithKline	67.	69	Mercer
18.	16	IBM	68.	77	Lehman Brothers
19.	17	JPMorgan	69.	50	Reuters
20.	25	BP	70.	89	GCHQ
21.	18	Unilever	71.	49	McDonald's Restaurants
22.	30	Marks & Spencer	72.	52	John Lewis
23.	24	Rolls-Royce	73.	84	Barclays Capital
24.	21	Microsoft	74.	82	Corus
25.	42	Morgan Stanley	75.	100	Credit Suisse
26.	35	Tesco	76.	94	Dstl
27.	20	Police	77.	65	Airbus
28.	26	L'Oréal	78.	87	Boston Consulting Group
29.	40	BT	79.	73	Slaughter and May
30.	38	McKinsey & Company	80.	93	Bloomberg
31.	47	UBS	81.	NEW	Fujitsu
32.	48	Mars	82.	98	Intel
33.	23	Deutsche Bank	83.	76	DLA Piper
34.	31	Citigroup	84.	88	Environment Agency
35.	28	Barclays Bank	85.	83	Ministry of Defence
36.	45	AstraZeneca	86.	79	British Airways
37.	34	Lloyds TSB	87.	96	Sony
38.	32	RAF	88.	NEW	Virgin
39.	33	Local Government	89.	81	Saatchi & Saatchi
40.	29	Clifford Chance	90.	62	Baker & McKenzie
41.	57	Allen & Overy	91.	80	Herbert Smith
42.	37	Sainsbury's	92.	64	Pfizer
43.	27	BAE Systems	93.	NEW	Financial Services Authority
44.	43	Linklaters	94.	70	Penguin
45.	53	Oxfam	95.	99	Siemens
46.	56	Boots	96.	NEW	Bank of America
47.	60	Cadbury Schweppes	97.	NEW	Government Legal Service
48.	55	QinetiQ	98.	NEW	Grant Thornton
49.	46	Diageo	99.	NEW	Nationwide
50.	54	Royal Navy	100.	NEW	Addleshaw Goddard

Source **The UK Graduate Careers Survey 2006**, High Fliers Research Ltd. 16,452 final year students leaving UK universities in the summer 2006 were asked 'Which employer do you think offers the best opportunities for graduates?'

from meeting employers' representatives, or experiences through the recruitment and selection process. Finalists also considered the numbers of vacancies that organisations were recruiting for as an indicator of graduates' prospects, or were influenced by an employer's profile on campus.

Many students, however, used the 'employment proposition' as their main guide – the quality of graduate training and development that an employer offers, the remuneration package available, and the practical aspects of a first job such as location or working hours.

Irrespective of the criteria that students used to arrive at their answer, the hardest part for many was just selecting a single organisation. In many ways, choosing two or three, or even half a dozen employers would have been much easier. But the whole purpose of the exercise was to replicate the reality that everyone faces – you can only work for one organisation. And at each stage of the job search there are choices to be made as to which direction to take and which employers to pursue.

The resulting *Top 100* is a dynamic league table of the UK's most exciting and well-respected graduate recruiters in 2006. For the third year running, the accounting & professional services firm, PricewaterhouseCoopers has been named Britain's number one graduate employer, polling more than 10 per cent of the total student vote.

For the first time since the *Top 100* was launched in 1997, the top three places in the employers league table are all taken by 'Big Four' professional services firms – Deloitte jump four places to 2nd and KPMG move up one place to 3rd.

As a result the Civil Service, a former Top 100 number one, has dropped from 2nd to 4th place. The BBC remain in the top five for the second year running, just ahead of the NHS in 6th place. Banking group HSBC has moved up to 7th position but Accenture has dropped five places to 8th, the consulting firm's lowest ranking for ten years.

Procter & Gamble remains the highest-ranking fast-moving consumer goods company and goes up one place to 9th, overtaking Goldman Sachs, the investment bank who are in 10th place this year.

Outside of the top ten, there have been a number of significant changes. Retailer Aldi jumps an impressive ten places to 12th, Teach First continue upwards to 16th place and BP move up five places to return to the top twenty for the first time in four years. Shell has also improved its position and is now ranked in 11th place.

The UK's largest public sector graduate recruiter, the Army, which dropped out of the top ten last year, falls another two places to 13th. Ernst & Young, the professional services firm and the Royal Bank of Scotland Group remain in 14th and 15th place for the third consecutive year. Unilever, the consumer goods company, has left the top twenty and is now ranked in 21st place.

The two highest climbers of the year in the *Top 100* were the internet company Google who moved up an impressive thirty-two positions to 53rd place, and IT firm Data Connection which jumped twenty-six places to 60th place. Heading in the wrong direction, the biggest falls of the year were for the international pharmaceuticals company Pfizer and law firm Baker & McKenzie which both dropped nearly thirty places in the league table.

The eleven investment banks listed in the *Top 100* enjoyed mixed fortunes in 2006 – Morgan Stanley, UBS and Credit Suisse were high climbers and both Lehman Brothers and Barclays Capital improved their positions. But JPMorgan, Deutsche Bank, Citigroup and Merrill Lynch each had lower rankings.

There was a similar picture amongst the leading law firms – Allen & Overy, Freshfields and Lovells each moved up the table, whilst Clifford Chance, Linklaters, Slaughter and May, Eversheds and Herbert Smith all slipped back a number of places.

There are a total of eight new entries in the new *Top 100*, the highest being IT and communications group Fujitsu in 81st place. The Financial Services Authority appear in 93rd place and the Bank of America, the Government Legal Service, accountancy firm Grant Thornton, Nationwide Building Society and law firm Addleshaw Goddard take the last five places in this year's list. Two employers return to the league table – Virgin in 88th place and Grant Thornton in 98th.

Among the organisations leaving the *Top 100* in 2006 are motor manufacturer Ford – a former top twenty employer, MI5 – The Security Service, British Nuclear Group and investment bank ABN Amro. Three of last year's new entries also failed to retain their places – PA Consulting, chemical giant ICI and law firm Simmons & Simmons.

It is now ten years since the first league table was produced and in that time there have been just four organisations at number one – retailer Marks & Spencer in 1997, Accenture (formerly Andersen Consulting) for five consecutive years from 1998 to 2002, the Civil Service in 2003, and now PricewaterhouseCoopers from 2004 to 2006.

This year's edition of *The Times Top 100 Graduate Employers* has produced a number of dramatic changes, particularly at the top of the list, and the results provide a unique insight into how graduates from the 'Class of 2006' rated the leading employers in 2005-2006. Many of these organisations are featured in the 'Employer Entry' section of this book. Starting on page 37, you can see a two-page profile for each employer, listed alphabetically for easy reference.

The editorial part of the entry includes a short description of what the organisation does, its opportunities for graduates and its recruitment programme for 2006-2007. A fact file for each employer gives details of the number of graduate vacancies, the business functions that graduates are recruited for, likely starting salaries for 2007, application deadlines, the universities that the employer is intending to visit during the year, and contact details for their recruitment website and graduate brochure. The right-hand page of the entry contains a display advert from the employer.

If you would like to find out more about any of the employers featured in *The Times Top 100 Graduate Employers*, then you can use the book's 'Information Request Service' – simply register your personal details and the employers you are interested in using the request card that appears opposite page 200, or go online to **www.Top100GraduateEmployers.com**

You'll receive email bulletins about the employers, details of their presentations and careers events at your university, and other information about their graduate recruitment. The service is entirely free and you choose which organisations you would like to hear about.

Using the 'Information Request Service' enters you into a prize draw to win **£5,000**. There are also 50 **iPod Nanos** to be won – one at each of the universities at which the *Top 100* book is distributed, for those who return their information request cards early, before **30th November 2006**.

THE TIMES TOP 100 GRADUATE EMPLOYERS

Employers in this year's Top 100

	Number of Employers			Number of Employers
1. Public Sector Employer	12	9.	Bank or Financial Institution	6
2. Investment Bank	11	10.	Accountancy or Professional Services Firm	5
3. Law Firm	11	11.	Consulting Firm	5
4. Retailer	9	12.	Armed Forces	3
5. Engineering or Industrial Company	8	13.	Oil Company	3
6. Fast-Moving Consumer Goods Company	8	14.	Chemical or Pharmaceutical Company	2
7. IT or Telecoms Company	7	15.	Charity or Voluntary Sector	2
8. Media Company	6	16.	Other	2

Source **The UK Graduate Careers Survey 2006**, High Fliers Research Ltd. 16,452 final year students leaving UK universities in the summer 2006 were asked 'Which employer do you think offers the best opportunities for graduates?'

Peter once imagined he could be Mr Universe.

Now he's proved his strength on the sale of Fitness First.

Ambition is a good thing. So are aspirations. Ours have helped to keep us ahead in the global marketplace for professional services. It's the ambition of exceptional individuals like you that has helped us achieve our goals. Like the expert valuation and unprecedented market insights we provided for this leisure group. For you, it's the promise of a career that can take you further - and faster - than you ever thought possible.

www.deloitte.co.uk/graduates

A career worth aspiring to

Deloitte.

Audit . Tax . Consulting . Corporate Finance .

How to use the directory

Many of the employers listed within The Times Top 100 Graduate Employers are featured in the 'Employer Entries' section of the directory. These entries describe what each organisation does, the opportunities they offer graduates, and practical details about their recruitment programme for 2006-2007.

The 'Employer Entry' section begins on page 37.

Each entry follows a standard format, and contains two elements: descriptive text and easy-to-find information on the employer's vacancies, contact details and salary expectations.

Locations of jobs
The regional locations of the employer's jobs are highlighted in red.

Vacancies
The number of likely graduate vacancies at this employer in 2006-2007

Employer's graduate recruitment website

Career areas recruited for
Details of the generic career areas that the employer recruits into. There are 17 areas to look out for:

- Accountancy
- Consultancy
- Engineering
- Finance
- General Management
- Human Resources
- Investment Banking
- IT
- Law
- Logistics
- Manufacturing
- Marketing
- Media
- Purchasing
- Research & Development
- Retailing
- Sales

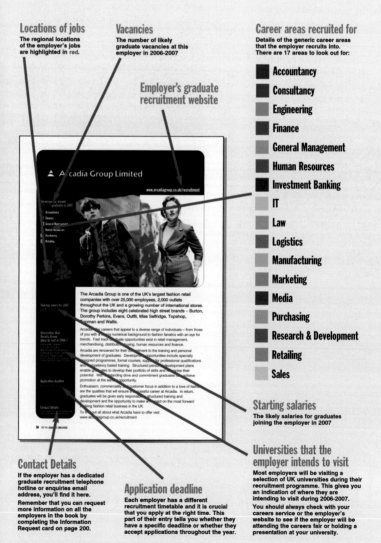

Starting salaries
The likely salaries for graduates joining the employer in 2007

Universities that the employer intends to visit
Most employers will be visiting a selection of UK universities during their recruitment programme. This gives you an indication of where they are intending to visit during 2006-2007. You should always check with your careers service or the employer's website to see if the employer will be attending the careers fair or holding a presentation at your university.

Contact Details
If the employer has a dedicated graduate recruitment telephone hotline or enquiries email address, you'll find it here.
Remember that you can request more information on all the employers in the book by completing the Information Request card on page 200.

Application deadline
Each employer has a different recruitment timetable and it is crucial that you apply at the right time. This part of their entry tells you whether they have a specific deadline or whether they accept applications throughout the year.

Henrietta
is a Crude Oil Freight Trader
with Shell in London

"With Shell behind you, your career can go a long way – and I was given excellent industry training right from the start. Next came 'Shell Life', the personal development programme held in Amsterdam with delegates from all over the world. I feel the company's working with me to develop the skills I need – both for my current role and for the future. At some point, I hope to move into an oil trading role, possibly in Houston or Singapore."

Shell is an Equal Opportunity Employer

www.shell.com/careers

Test it

The strength of
our commitment

Achieving more together

The

world

The Mars Management Development Programme is business training and then some. It's unashamedly exclusive for stars-in-the-making. Our galaxy of past 'graduates' includes CEOs, Chairmen, company Presidents and even a Lord. Visit www.mars.com/ultimategrads for more. A lot more.

is

not

enough.

CAREER

Appointments ... plus a weekly guide to enhancing your value 29.06.06

INSIDE: THE BEST JOBS

THE TIMES

THURSDAYS

RECRUITMENT A profession that aims to attract high achievers 8
▶ No bull: do you have what takes to become a head...

THE JOB Drive time: self-starters find the gears to go further 3
▶ Pass master: don't be intimidated when facing a psychometric test 4

MANAGEMENT Break a leg: doe superstition belong at work? 4
▶ The feelgood factor: why money won't always motivate managers 6

Critical Roles – Music Industry

Understanding the Graduate Market

by Carol Lewis
Editor, Career - The Times

Markets are all about buying and selling and the graduate jobs market is no different. And just as need and desirability are drivers for our purchases in the high street, so they play their role in the department store of graduate jobs. Employers, who want to hire university leavers, need to make themselves desirable to graduates. Graduates, who want to be hired, need to make themselves desirable to employers. The ideal market for graduates is lots of employers who want to hire lots of bright university leavers. The best market situation for employers is lots of bright university leavers looking for jobs.

In the last ten years the number of people graduating from university has increased by almost 100,000 and in 2006 there were about 260,000 graduates. For these 260,000 people there were estimated to be between 85,000 and 90,000 graduate level vacancies. A quick bit of arithmetic shows that is the equivalent of one job for every three graduates. Of course not everyone wants a graduate job – some will want to travel, study, volunteer or find employment in roles which aren't strictly graduate jobs. Nonetheless getting a good graduate job at a top employer isn't easy, with each vacancy currently attracting between 25 and 100 applications.

The good news is that graduate vacancies at *The Times Top 100 Employers* are set to increase by 9 per cent this year – it is the fourth year running that the number of new graduate positions has increased. Together the employers featured in this year's *Top 100* are planning to hire 16,480 graduates, compared to the 15,120 recruited during 2005-2006.

The average number of graduate vacancies at *Top 100* employers is now 100 per organisation. One in six of the employers are set to hire at least 250 new recruits and four of the top 100 employers anticipate employing at least 1,000 university leavers this year. More than a third of the leading recruiters plan to hire more graduates this year than last, half believe they will recruit similar numbers to 2006, while just one in ten expects to reduce their graduate intake in 2007.

This is all good news, particularly for those with a head for figures. Most of the vacancies are at accountancy firms – 24.9 per cent of total graduate jobs, or investment banks – 19.3 per cent of total. Don't panic if you are an arts graduate though: almost all the big professional services firms and financial institutions say they want to recruit people from a broad range of degree backgrounds – they are not looking to hire ready-made accountants and bankers.

But if these sectors don't appeal there are also plenty of graduate vacancies in the public sector (14.9 per cent of the total for 2007) and industry (7.4 per cent). The employers who intend to take on the fewest new recruits are in the chemicals & pharmaceuticals sector

far-reaching
careers in finance

Five-year Finance Leader Development Programme
Starting salary £25,000

Set your sights beyond CIMA qualification. BAE Systems is behind tomorrow's defence technology. And our five-year Finance Leader Development Programme (FLDP) aims to develop our next generation of Finance Directors.

We're a 'CIMA Training Quality Partner'. So you'll gain all-round financial, leadership and business expertise. You'll work on real projects. And you'll have all the tools to perform at your best. But you'll need to be resilient and analytical, with a hands-on approach to finance.

Find out more about our projects and requirements. Go to **www.graduates-baesystems.com** from where you can apply online. Or call 01772 677277 for a copy of our brochure.

BAE Systems' technology sits at the heart of the F-35 Joint Strike Fighter, the largest defence programme in the world.

CIMA
TRAINING QUALITY PARTNER

BAE SYSTEMS

(0.4 per cent of total graduate jobs), consumer goods (1.4 per cent of total), and oil & energy (2.1 per cent of total).

The fastest growing sectors are investment banking, where graduate vacancies are up by over a fifth compared with 2006, other banking and financial employers and engineering & industrial companies. Media firms, IT & telecoms companies, and oil & energy companies also plan to recruit more graduates in 2007, but vacancies at accountancy & professional services firms, public sector employers, law firms and retailers are largely unchanged from 2006 levels. Just two sectors are predicting a smaller graduate intake this year than last – consumer goods manufacturers and management consulting firms.

In 2005, the majority of chief executives of FTSE-100 organisations, the UK's largest companies, came from a background of working in financial management according to a study by Dr Elizabeth Marx, a partner at headhunters Heidrick and Struggles, which suggests the current crop of graduate jobs really could be the first rung on the ladder to a stellar career.

The biggest graduate recruiters in *The Times Top 100 Graduate Employers* in 2007 are PricewaterhouseCoopers and Deloitte (1,200 vacancies each), the Army and Deutsche Bank (1,000 vacancies each), KPMG (850 vacancies), Ernst & Young (650 vacancies), Bloomberg (600 vacancies), and Accenture, Barclays Capital, HSBC and JP Morgan (400 vacancies each).

More than half of the *Top 100* companies have graduate vacancies in financial management and IT, a third offer jobs in human resources and marketing, a quarter of employers are hiring graduate engineers or sales staff, general managers or research & development personnel.

Only seven out of the *Top 100* employers have media vacancies. The media is always one of the most desirable career destinations for

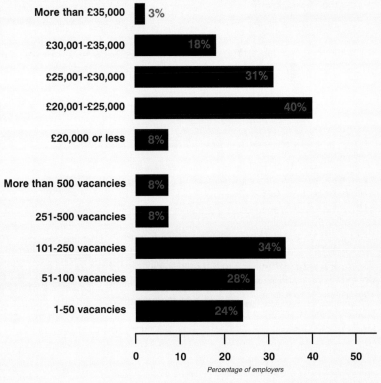

Graduate Salaries & Vacancies in 2007

More than £35,000	3%
£30,001-£35,000	18%
£25,001-£30,000	31%
£20,001-£25,000	40%
£20,000 or less	8%
More than 500 vacancies	8%
251-500 vacancies	8%
101-250 vacancies	34%
51-100 vacancies	28%
1-50 vacancies	24%

Percentage of employers

Source **The Times Top 100 Graduate Employers 2006-7**, High Fliers Research Ltd. Average graduate starting salaries and total number of graduate vacancies in 2007 at the organisations featured in The Times Top 100 Graduate Employers.

graduates, this suggests that graduates intent on pursuing media careers would do well to consider applying to employers outside the *Top 100* or looking for vacancies that are not specifically classified as graduate jobs.

The survey by High Fliers Research of more than 16,000 final year students expecting to graduate in 2006 that is used to compile the latest *Top 100* league table showed that most wanted to work in London and the south of England. Let's hope the same is true in 2007 because three-quarters of leading employers are recruiting graduates to work in the capital and more than half have vacancies in the south east of England or the Midlands this year. By contrast, less than half have any vacancies in Scotland, Wales or Northern Ireland. About a third of employers are offering jobs in the north west, south west, Yorkshire or the north east of England. The region with the fewest graduate employers is East Anglia.

It goes without saying that everyone wants an interesting and satisfying career but the fiscal reality is that with the average student leaving university £10,000 in debt, salaries do matter. Luckily the UK's leading graduate employers are set to boost starting salaries by 7.8 per cent in 2007 – one of the highest rises ever recorded, taking average packages to £26,400. This is a £1,900 increase on last year's average graduate starting salary.

The highest starting salary published by this year's *Top 100* employers is £38,000 which is being offered by retailer Aldi. More than a fifth of the top graduate programmes will now pay graduates at least £30,000 when they start work later this year. The most generous salaries tend to be those on offer from investment banks (an average of £35,000), law firms (average £30,000), and consulting firms (average £28,500), although these rates are largely unchanged on 2006 rates.

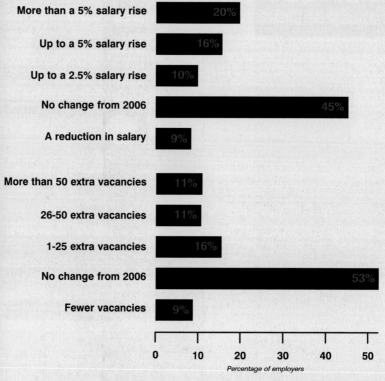

Changes to Salaries & Vacancies in 2007

	Percentage of employers
More than a 5% salary rise	20%
Up to a 5% salary rise	16%
Up to a 2.5% salary rise	10%
No change from 2006	45%
A reduction in salary	9%
More than 50 extra vacancies	11%
26-50 extra vacancies	11%
1-25 extra vacancies	16%
No change from 2006	53%
Fewer vacancies	9%

Source **The Times Top 100 Graduate Employers 2006-7**, High Fliers Research Ltd. Graduate starting salaries & vacancy levels in 2007, compared with recruitment in 2006 at the organisations featured in The Times Top 100 Graduate Employers

Getinsidebusiness

Build better business from the inside.
Explore a career with Ernst & Young.

www.ey.com/uk/graduate

ERNST & YOUNG

Quality In Everything We Do

At the other end of the scale eight organisations plan to pay initial salaries of £20,000 or less to graduates. Despite the problem of rising student debt though these organisations are still well worth considering. There is much more to life than money – you really need to consider what motivates you, what career development and training opportunities are available, the work-life balance you want and your long-term career strategies.

The majority of leading employers are not that hard to find: most of the companies featured in *The Times Top 100 Employers* are actively marketing their graduate vacancies at between 10 and 20 UK universities during 2006-2007. Recruiters use a variety of careers fairs, campus recruitment presentations and media advertising. The five universities that are likely to be most often targeted by Britain's leading graduate employers during this recruitment season are Manchester, Cambridge, Nottingham, Warwick and London.

But if the company you'd most like to work for hasn't visited your university then don't despair, log on instead. Every leading employer has their own recruitment website which gives full details about their graduate programmes, case studies of recent joiners, their training & development and online applications systems.

Half of the UK's *Top 100* employers now recruit all year-round and plan to accept applications throughout the 2006-2007 recruitment season. For employers with a single application deadline, the most common deadlines are in November or December, although most major law firms usually have July deadlines.

To recap, there are lots of reasons to feel positive about life after graduation – vacancies for university leavers have now risen by over a third since 2004 and starting salaries have increased by a spectacular 14 per cent over the same period.

No one can expect to walk into a job; there is tough competition for all vacancies and the leading employers have rigorous selection procedures. Graduates not only need a good degree – most *Top 100* employers want to recruit those with a first or 2.1 – but also must demonstrate a range of skills and business acumen. Employers crave well-rounded individuals with demonstrable competencies such as effective communication, motivation and organisation, the ability to work in teams and leadership potential.

But for those finalists who do make the grade there are rewarding careers and excellent salaries on offer from Britain's best-known and most sought-after graduate employers.

'Career' is the weekly jobs section published every Thursday in The Times – www.timesonline.co.uk/career

THE TIMES TOP 100 GRADUATE EMPLOYERS

Graduate Employment in 2007, by Industry

	2006		% of total vacancies in 2007	How graduate vacancies compare with 2006
1.	1	**Accountancy or Professional Services Firms**	24.9	Up 2.5%
2.	2	**Investment Banks or Fund Managers**	19.3	Up 21.2%
3.	3	**Public Sector**	14.9	Up 2.1%
4.	4	**Engineering or Industrial Companies**	7.4	Up 7.5%
5.	7	**Banking or Financial Services**	6.3	Up 18.8%
6.	5	**Law Firms**	6.1	Up 1.5%
7.	6	**Retailers**	5.5	Up 1.1%
8.	9	**IT & Telecommunications Companies**	4.2	Up 46.8%
9.	10	**Media Organisations**	3.9	Up 66.7%
10.	8	**Consulting Firms**	2.9	Down 23.8%
11.	11	**Oil & Energy Companies**	2.1	Up 25.9%
12.	12	**Consumer Goods Manufacturers**	1.4	Down 7.8%
13.	13	**Chemical & Pharmaceuticals**	0.4	No change
14.	-	**Other**	0.7	No change

Source **The Times Top 100 Graduate Employers 2006-7**, High Fliers Research Ltd. Graduate vacancy levels in 2007, compared with total numbers recruited in 2006 at the organisations featured in The Times Top 100 Graduate Employers

limitless potential

[MERRILL LYNCH]

growth and momentum
inspiring colleagues

Merrill Lynch offers you unparalleled opportunities to build your career. Our premier brand and global capabilities create a strong foundation for you to explore a range of diverse career options. Working within a dynamic environment, you will contribute to our company's business growth and momentum. It's a great time to join us.

Work alongside industry-leading professionals to deliver exceptional solutions to our clients. Expect to be a contributor, a collaborator, and a colleague.

We can offer you a world-class introduction to international debt and equity products in Global Markets; advisory and capital markets and financing services through Investment Banking; to macro and securities analysis through Research and systems development, business analysis and project management in Technology.

For more information or to apply online, visit

ml.com/careers/europe

Merrill Lynch is an equal opportunity employer.

ml.com/careers/europe

For invaluable career advice consult your newsagent

With pages of graduate jobs – and expert advice to help you get them – this is the definitive guide to taking control of your career.

Read Career, only in The Times every Thursday.

For the latest career news, advice and job searches, go to timesonline.co.uk/career

CAREER

INSIDE: THE BEST JOBS

Appointments . . . plus a weekly guide to enhancing your value 08.12.05

THE TIMES
THURSDAYS
www.timesonline.co.uk/career

THE JOB Go ape: how to become a special effects technician 4
▶ Summer school: our guide to the internships available next year 5

MANAGEMENT Jingle hell: what it takes to survive Christmas 4
▶ Sound advice: get a mini music centre to liven up your workspace 6

GRADUATES Custom kit: tailor your benefits to fit your needs 3
▶ Why Chinese women students choose British business schools 6

Resolve the conflict by discussing the issue?

Ignore the conflict and hope it goes away?

To ensure you're better prepared to make tough decisions, call the Chartered Management Institute on 0845 053 0403 or visit managers.org.uk/2005

chartered
management
institute

inspiring leaders

Successful Job Hunting

by Jeff Goodman
Director, Careers Advisory Service
University of Bristol

Some students have known for a very long time exactly which career to pursue and arrive in their first year at university convinced that they want to work in accountancy or are interested in broadcasting. But for many, "I don't have clue, where do I start?" is a much more likely position when it comes to thinking about what to do after graduation.

Help is at hand, though, as every university in the UK has its own careers service to assist university-leavers with the transition into the working world. Their purpose is to encourage students to understand the opportunities that are available, guide them to make appropriate decisions about their future and then assist with implementing a successful job search. Providing inspiration is an important part of the services' role too – getting people fired-up and interested in what they could be doing after their degree.

The earlier you can make a first visit to your careers service or look at their website the better. The whole process of working out what you want to do, getting the right experience and skills can be quite lengthy, especially if you don't have a good understanding of the graduate job market.

Most careers services have comprehensive libraries with reference material on a wide range of occupations and job types, as well as a wealth of online information such as latest vacancies, events information, email bulletins and career podcasts. A typical large university will have between 3,000 and 4,000 local, regional, national and international employers register graduate job vacancies with the careers service each year.

Many careers services offer the *Prospects Planner* system, a computer-aided guidance program which helps identify the occupations that relate to your interests skills and values. It won't tell you exactly which job you should do but it will suggest possible areas for you to consider. Another useful resource is the alumni lists – contact details for a number of the university's former students. These are graduates who are happy to share their experiences of employment with current students and offer advice either via email, telephone or sometimes in person.

All university careers services have a team of careers advisers who offer first hand advice on job hunting. Most now offer 'drop-in' sessions, informal consultations of around 15 minutes which don't need to be pre-booked. The aim is to make advisers available to as many students as possible for short discussions or specific enquiries.

These 'drop-in' sessions can be an excellent starting point for your job hunting. Advisers will try to get a feel for the ideas you have about possible career options, the areas you've considered and the things you've already rejected. They'll typically check what you're good at, what you've done at university and whether any of your work experience has

A sound investment in your future

ACA – the qualification for business leaders

If you want to make a sound investment in your future, then the ACA qualification from the ICAEW will provide you with the foundation for a successful career.

Chartered accountants are leading the way in many of the world's largest companies and are widely regarded as the advisers and influencers of leading organisations.

To get the facts and discover the opportunities about the qualification for business leaders, go to:

Web: **www.icaew.co.uk/careers**
Email: **times@icaew.co.uk**
Tel: **+44 (0)1908 24 8040**

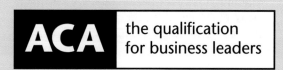

ACA — the qualification for business leaders

LPDADV5271

revealed the kinds of jobs you might enjoy in the future. The extent to which your degree subject is important to you is quite a key measure because that can really sharpen the focus of prospective job choices. From all of this, advisers can begin to tease out your real aims and motivations and, crucially, set out a plan of action in terms of the further research you need to do to find out about different types of work and occupations.

What career advisers cannot do is make your choices for you. A lot of students assume that advisers have all the answers and hope that by asking 'What should I do?' they'll get a specific solution. That isn't an adviser's role – they are there to guide you through the decision-making process and help you formulate your own ideas.

For those who need more time than a 'drop-in' session provides, many services offer longer, one hour consultations, which may be booked in advance and are likely to cover similar issues but give the adviser more of an opportunity to explore your ideas and get to know the issues that are important to you. These extended sessions may well be more useful further into the job-hunting process when you've gathered more information about your options.

Once you start to formulate a clearer notion of which areas you are interested in, you can begin finding out about individual organisations. Much of this specific information can be found on employers' own websites or in their recruitment brochures and these are a good source of facts and figures about the organisation and its graduate programme.

To get a proper understanding of what an employer is offering, though, you really need to meet them in person either at a careers fair or campus presentation. At the large universities, its not unusual to have a number of different recruitment fairs take place during the year but there's often one larger general event held during the autumn, supported with events for individual career areas such as law, engineering or IT.

The fairs can be an excellent opportunity to have conversations with a range of employers, albeit fairly brief ones. These discussions are more useful if you've done some research, so simply wandering round the stands in a casual way may not be much use. Very few employers respond well to being asked 'What can you tell me? What can you offer me?' – you need to give

some thought as to why you're going to speak to them and what to ask.

Campus presentations offer a fuller experience and there can be up to two hundred employer events during the autumn, depending on your university. Apart from the official description about what the company does, presentations may give you the chance to talk to recent graduates. Although they may seem primed to say the right things, you do get an impression of what they like about their job and the culture of the company, which can be really helpful, even at quite an early stage. They're invaluable if you're thinking 'Shall I be an accountant or go into marketing?' – you can very quickly get a sense of what feels right for you and where you belong.

Having seen a number of employers in person, you can then plan your application strategy. The clearer you can be about what you're looking for, the more likely you are to be able to distinguish between individual employers. It's a truism in graduate recruitment that almost everyone when asked why they applied to a company or why did they accept an offer, will say was because of the people – either because they were particularly friendly or impressive.

There's no easy answer about how many applications to make. In the past, students who have applied to just one company have been successful and yet others who applied to fifty haven't managed to get anywhere at all. For mainstream graduate programmes, completing ten applications may well be sufficient but it's largely down to the industry you're interested in. If you are hoping to work in one of the most competitive areas such as investment banking or consulting, you may want to think about applying to other areas too, as a possible fall-back.

The really important thing – and it is becoming more and more essential every year – is to make sure that your applications are of a high quality. In a more competitive market, there's simply no point in making dozens of fairly casual applications in the hope that one of them will hit home because most recruiters are very good at judging how motivated someone is and whether they've researched things carefully.

Before you launch into individual applications, it can be very useful to prepare a CV. Although many of the most popular employers will insist you complete their own online application, compiling a CV is a very good way for you to identify the sort of core of information that all applications will require and to remind yourself of what you've got to offer. You should describe your educational experience, outline any work experience and explain any other interests and activities that could be to your advantage. If you are going to use the CV to make applications, bear in mind that many employers will often spend less than a minute reviewing it, so it has to be really clear and concise.

Turning all this information into a meaningful application for individual employers can be quite a challenge but it is something that your careers service will be able to help you with. A good understanding of the employer and their business is a must – they will have gone to considerable lengths to produce a brochure or website to explain the skills they are looking for – and your application must be able to demonstrate how you match these requirements.

Many applications will also ask you to draw significance out of your experiences to demonstrate, for example, how you convinced someone else to do something or how you've worked effectively in a team or solved certain problems. The answers to these questions may not flow easily initially but a career adviser can help you come up with the concrete examples that employers are looking for.

If all goes well and your application is accepted then the next stage is likely to be a first interview. This may be a face-to-face meeting but increasingly employers are using telephone interviews to pre-screen candidates too. Keep a copy of your original application – it's important to be really familiar with what you have said already so you can practice how you might discuss things in the interview.

In simple terms, what the employers are looking for are answers to the questions: "Why are you interested in that job with the company?" and "Why should they be interested in you?". They are likely to ask the first of these straight out and will expect you to have a good idea of what you would do at the company, where that would lead and why you think your skills match those you'd be using in the job. That's really about motivation and showing your application to them was based on some genuine research.

It's one thing to demonstrate why an employer should be interested in you in writing, but it's another thing entirely to do it under verbal questioning. You need to have really thought through what examples you'll use and how you can prove you are what they're looking for. The questions could be as bald as "Tell me how you worked in a team?" or it could be less obvious: "Describe something you're really proud of" followed up with "How did it work, how much was it down to you, how much did you collaborate with others?". There are all sorts of oblique ways of digging down to the same thing.

Many careers services run workshops on interview training. These could provide you with experience of interviewing other participants and being interviewed by them, under the guidance of an expert. Alternatively, you could book an interview practice session, which are run either as a small group or on a one-to-one basis, depending on your university.

For those who are successful at interview, the final selection round is likely to be a one or two-day assessment centre with ability or personality tests, group exercises and further interviews. It is well worth practicing the ability tests, as their format may be quite unlike anything you've encountered before. Websites such as Saville & Holdsworth offer free online tests and many careers services have examples of tests used by recruiters and some services offer practice test sessions. The more practice you get the more familiar and relaxed you are likely to be when you take them for real.

The group activities at assessment centres are often task-focused which means you and the other applicants are set challenges to collaborate on, while assessors observe how you interact in the group. In this situation, remember that most companies are looking to recruit a range of different personalities and characters. As well as natural leaders and organisers, they need people who generate ideas or analyse situations and others to take supporting roles. Therefore, there is no single 'right way' to come across during the exercises. Try and be yourself and play to your own particular strengths, rather than striving to be a 'great leader' if that isn't you.

Remember too that this stage of selection often includes a social element and though this may not be formally assessed it is still an integral part of the process. Recent graduates often join

IN STOCK...

CONSULTANT

LAWYER

CHEMIST

MANAGER

JOURNALIST

SALES

ENGINEER

PR

PROGRAMMER

TEACHER

FINANCE

BANKER

ANALYST

ACCOUNTANT

TECHNICIAN

candidates over lunch or dinner and can appear very helpful and friendly but just be aware their opinions may be important – they could also be useful sources of information for you.

If you do win through and receive a job offer at the end of the recruitment round, your final challenge is whether to accept or not. Don't feel pressured into making a snap decision – employers naturally want to grab someone that they like and get you committed. But you may want time to weigh up your options or you might still be waiting to hear the outcome of other applications you've made. Different organisations work to different recruitment timetables and most employers will recognise that they may have to wait for your decision. Be as honest and straightforward with them as possible and let them know what your position is.

If you've got a few offers to choose from it is always helpful to talk things through with a careers adviser. Think back to your original priorities and try and be clear about what you are looking for. Sometimes the issue is "this is the job that I want" but "that other one pays more money" – it's a tough dilemma but immediate starting salaries don't necessarily tell the whole story about what you could be earning in the future.

On the whole, if you are doing something you really enjoy then you're more likely to do it well, which means you're going to create a good impression, your managers, colleagues and customers are going to be impressed and you will

be more successful – it's a virtuous circle. So if it's a choice between doing something you love and something that appears to have more status or more money, think very carefully about where you will really flourish.

Not everyone, though, will get a job offer from their first batch of applications. If you have been rejected outright at application stage, it may be time to get some more help with the way you present yourself or re-examine which career areas to pursue before you make another round of applications. If you have had an interview and certainly if you've been to a selection centre, recruiters are sometimes prepared to explain why they didn't choose you and offer advice about where you can improve.

Lack of work experience is likely to be one of the main reasons why applicants aren't successful so it may be worth thinking about applying for a summer placement instead and then re-applying for graduate schemes later in the year after you've graduated.

Whatever the outcome of your job hunting as an undergraduate, most careers services will continue to support you for a time after you complete your degree, which means you'll have free access to the careers service and all its facilities in person, through e-guidance and via the website. You may also be able to get help from local universities elsewhere in the country although there may be a charge to use their careers service or consult their careers advisers.

THE TIMES TOP 100 GRADUATE EMPLOYERS

Leading Destinations for 2006 Graduates

	% who wanted to work in sector		% who wanted to work in sector
1. Media	12.4	11. Law	6.6
2. Teaching	11.9	12. Human Resources	6.2
3. Investment Banking	11.1	13. General Management	5.3
4. Marketing	11.0	14. IT	5.2
5. Accountancy	10.8	15. Sales	4.9
6. Consulting	10.3	16. Retailing	3.9
7. Research & Development	9.8	17. Armed Forces	3.1
8. Charity or Voluntary Work	8.6	18. Buying or Purchasing	2.6
9. Civil Service	8.5	19. Property	2.4
10. Engineering	7.5	20. Police	2.1

Source **The UK Graduate Careers Survey 2006**, High Fliers Research Ltd. 16,452 final year students leaving who left UK universities in the summer of 2006 were asked which sectors they had applied to or planned to apply to for a graduate job.

..ALL THE BEST GRADUATE JOBS

Right now you're working hard to get your degree but have you worked out your next step yet?

If you're looking to launch a fantastic career when you graduate, Milkround Online has lots of resources to help you do so.

- **Milkround.com features hundreds of graduate vacancies at leading firms.**
- **Information about upcoming application deadlines, and events such as recruitment fairs and open days.**
- **Regular email alerts and industry e-zines with opportunities in your chosen area.**

So to make your first step in the world of work the right one, head to **www.milkround.com** today and see what's on offer!

THE TIMES
TOP 100
GRADUATE EMPLOYERS

	Page		Page		Page
Accenture	40	Dstl	98	Mercer HR Consulting	150
Addleshaw Goddard	42	Ernst & Young	100	Merrill Lynch	152
Airbus	44	Eversheds	102	Metropolitan Police	154
Aldi	46	ExxonMobil	104	Microsoft	156
Allen & Overy	48	Financial Services		Ministry of Defence	158
Arcadia	50	Authority	106	Morgan Stanley	160
Army	52	Freshfields Bruckhaus		Nationwide	162
ASDA	54	Deringer	108	NGDP for	
AstraZeneca	56	Fujitsu	110	Local Government	164
Atkins	58	GCHQ	112	NHS	166
BAE Systems	60	GlaxoSmithKline	114	Oxfam	168
Baker & McKenzie	62	Goldman Sachs	116	Police - High Potential	
Barclays Bank	64	Google	118	Development Scheme	170
Barclays Capital	66	Grant Thornton	120	PricewaterhouseCoopers	172
BBC	68	HBOS	122	Procter & Gamble	174
Bloomberg	70	HSBC	124	QinetiQ	176
BP	72	IBM	126	Reuters	178
BT	74	John Lewis	128	Rolls-Royce	180
Cadbury Schweppes	76	JPMorgan	130	Royal Bank of	
Cancer Research UK	78	KPMG	132	Scotland Group	182
Citigroup	80	L'Oréal	134	Sainsbury's	184
Civil Service Fast Stream	82	Linklaters	136	Shell	186
Clifford Chance	84	Lloyds TSB	138	Slaughter and May	188
Corus	86	Lovells	140	Teach First	190
Credit Suisse	88	Marks & Spencer	142	Tesco	192
Data Connection	90	Mars	144	UBS	194
Deloitte	92	McDonald's Restaurants	146	Unilever	196
Deutsche Bank	94	McKinsey & Company	148	WPP	198
DLA Piper	96				

Index

	Accountancy	Consulting	Engineering	Finance	General Management	Human Resources	Investment Banking	IT	Law	Logistics	Manufacturing	Marketing	Media	Purchasing	Research & Development	Retailing	Sales	Other
Accenture		●						●										
Addleshaw Goddard									●									
Airbus			●	●		●		●		●	●			●				
Aldi Stores																●		
Allen & Overy									●									
Arcadia	●				●							●		●				
Army	●		●		●	●		●	●		●			●			●	
ASDA				●	●	●		●			●			●		●		
AstraZeneca			●					●			●			●	●			
Atkins		●	●															
BAE Systems			●	●	●	●					●			●	●			●
Baker & McKenzie									●									
Barclays Bank	●			●	●	●		●				●					●	●
Barclays Capital				●			●	●										
BBC	●		●	●					●			●	●		●			
Bloomberg				●				●					●		●		●	●
BP			●	●				●								●		
BT		●	●	●	●	●						●		●	●		●	
Cadbury Schweppes	●		●	●						●	●	●			●		●	
Cancer Research UK												●			●			
Citigroup						●	●	●										
Civil Service Fast Stream					●			●										
Clifford Chance									●									
Corus			●	●		●					●			●	●			●
Credit Suisse				●			●	●										
Data Connection								●										
Deloitte	●	●		●				●										
Deutsche Bank				●		●	●	●										
DLA Piper									●									
Dstl		●													●			
Ernst & Young	●	●		●		●												
Eversheds									●									
ExxonMobil			●	●	●			●			●						●	
Financial Services Authority			●	●														
Freshfields Bruckhaus Deringer									●									
Fujitsu	●	●	●		●	●		●				●		●			●	
GCHQ					●			●										
GlaxoSmithKline	●		●	●				●			●			●	●		●	
Goldman Sachs	●			●		●	●	●										
Google		●			●			●				●	●					●

	Accountancy	Consulting	Engineering	Finance	General Management	Human Resources	Investment Banking	IT	Law	Logistics	Manufacturing	Marketing	Media	Purchasing	Research & Development	Retailing	Sales	Other
Grant Thornton	●																	
HBOS				●	●	●	●	●				●				●	●	
HSBC				●	●		●	●		●						●	●	
IBM		●	●					●		●				●			●	
John Lewis															●			
JPMorgan							●	●										
KPMG	●	●		●		●		●				●					●	
L'Oréal			●									●		●			●	
Linklaters									●									
Lloyds TSB	●			●	●			●										
Lovells									●									
Marks & Spencer					●											●		
Mars			●	●	●							●			●		●	
McDonald's Restaurants					●											●		
McKinsey & Company		●																
Mercer HR Consulting		●	●															
Merrill Lynch				●			●	●						●				
Metropolitan Police																		●
Microsoft		●						●				●		●			●	
Ministry of Defence			●		●			●						●				
Morgan Stanley				●			●	●										
Nationwide				●		●		●							●			
NGDP for Local Government					●													
NHS				●	●	●												
Oxfam	●			●	●	●		●				●	●		●	●		
Police HPDS																		●
PricewaterhouseCoopers	●	●		●					●									
Procter & Gamble	●		●	●	●	●		●			●	●		●	●		●	
QinetiQ			●		●			●						●				
Reuters	●			●				●					●					
Rolls-Royce			●	●				●			●			●			●	
Royal Bank of Scotland Group	●	●		●		●	●	●								●	●	
Sainsbury's				●	●			●			●	●		●	●			
Shell			●	●				●				●			●		●	
Slaughter and May									●									
Teach First	●	●	●	●	●	●	●	●	●	●	●	●	●		●	●	●	
Tesco				●	●			●		●		●	●	●	●	●	●	
UBS				●		●	●	●		●								
Unilever			●		●			●				●					●	
WPP												●	●					

accenture

High performance. Delivered.

Vacancies for around 400 **graduates in 2007**

■ Consulting

■ IT

Starting salary for 2007
£28,500
Plus £10,000 bonus.

Universities Accenture plans to visit in 2006-7
Aston, Bath, Birmingham, Bristol, Cambridge, Cardiff, City, Durham, Edinburgh, Exeter, Glasgow, Lancaster, Leeds, Leicester, London, Loughborough, Manchester, Newcastle, Nottingham, Oxford, Sheffield, Southampton, St Andrews, Strathclyde, Swansea, Warwick
Please check with your university careers service for details of events.

Application deadline
Year-round recruitment

Contact Details
✉ ukgraduates@accenture.com
☎ 0500 100 189
Turn to page 200 now to request more information about Accenture.

With over 133,000 people working in 48 countries, Accenture is one of the world's leading management consulting, technology services and outsourcing organisations. They help their clients become high-performance businesses by delivering innovation and their work invariably involves the application of information technology to business challenges.

Accenture believe that they offer great opportunities for graduates, partly because of the work they do, and partly because learning and personal development are so high on their agenda. Graduates control their own development and promotion is based entirely on the skills they acquire and the contribution they make. Whilst flexible working programmes allow them to manage their schedule to suit them. They also actively encourage people to get involved in community and charitable activities that make a real difference to communities across the UK and around the world.

All graduates join Accenture's Graduate Training Programme in one of four areas: Business & Systems Integration Consulting, Technology Consulting, Business Consulting and Accenture's Outsourcing function. Find out more online.

Accenture look for people with more than just excellent academics. They need individuals who are passionate about something outside their studies, who have some work experience and a strong interest in business and technology. For graduates who meet the above criteria, expect to achieve a 2:1 degree and have 320 UCAS points, they can offer a truly rounded career.

Head start.
High performers start here.

Go on. Be a Tiger.

Accenture knows the importance of creating the right environment for success. We're one of the world's leading management consulting, technology services and outsourcing companies and we want talented people who are looking for a challenge. We offer unrivalled training and you'll be able to develop your skills faster here than almost anywhere else. Join our global team and you'll be delivering the innovation that helps our clients become high-performance businesses.

Graduate Careers in Consulting

Almost everything we do involves the application of IT to business challenges. But that's not to say you have to be a computer genius to get on here (although we certainly wouldn't hold it against you). If you're genuinely interested in business and technology, expect to achieve a 2:1 degree and have 320 UCAS points, we can offer you a truly rounded career.

As well as doing interesting, challenging work with exceptional people, and using the latest technology, you'll be rewarded well with a salary of £28,500 and an additional £10,000 bonus. We also actively encourage people to get involved in community and charitable activities that make a real difference to communities across the UK and around the world.

For people with the right intelligence and personal qualities, consulting is possibly the best job in the world. To find out more, and to apply, visit our website. Accenture is committed to being an equal opportunities employer.

Visit accenture.com/ukgraduates

• Consulting • Technology • Outsourcing

> accenture
High performance. Delivered.

ADDLESHAW GODDARD

www.addleshawgoddard.com/graduates

Vacancies for around
50 **graduates in 2007**

For training contracts starting in 2009

 Law

Starting salary for 2007
£Competitive

Universities that Addleshaw Goddard plans to visit in 2006-7

Bristol, Cambridge, Durham,
Exeter, Leeds, London,
Manchester, Nottingham,
Oxford, Sheffield,
St Andrews, York

Please check with your university careers service for details of events.

Application deadline
31st July 2007

Contact Details

✉ grad@addleshawgoddard.com

Turn to page 200 now to request more information about Addleshaw Goddard.

A leading national law firm with the capability to provide excellent service to a global client base. Ranked 16th largest law firm in the UK, Addleshaw Goddard is also ranked in The Sunday Times 100 Best Companies to work for.

The firm has four main practice areas: corporate, finance and projects, real estate and contentious and commercial.

Addleshaw Goddard are looking for graduates and undergraduates from any academic discipline who possess the motivation and commitment necessary to join a top 20 law firm and who are capable of achieving, or have achieved, at least a 2(i) degree.

During their training contract, trainees will be given the opportunity to experience a broad range of corporate and commercial work. During each six-month seat they will have regular performance reviews with their supervisor, and the on-the-job training will be supported by courses provided by the firm's in-house team and external experts.

Tuition fees are paid for both GDL and LPC courses, together with an annual maintenance grant – currently £7,000 per course for all future trainees studying the GDL or LPC in central London, and £4,500 per course for all future trainees studying elsewhere.

They have vacation schemes in their London, Leeds and Manchester offices both at Easter and Summer. For an invaluable insight into the firm and help deciding whether Addleshaw Goddard is the right destination, visit www.addleshawgoddard.com/graduates.

ADDLESHAW GODDARD

EAGER

Help us grow as a team.
We'll help you grow as an individual.
As a fast expanding and innovative law firm, a career with Addleshaw Goddard means more variety, earlier responsibility and greater future opportunities to develop with the firm. Training with us will mean working with top FTSE companies and other leading organisations.

But it's not just about hard work. We care about maintaining a balanced culture. The proof: our support for employees has resulted in *The Sunday Times* listing Addleshaw Goddard as one of its 'Top 100 Best Companies To Work For' in 2006.

With offices in London, Leeds and Manchester, we can offer quality training wherever you want to be based. If you are interested in a training contract with us or a Summer/Easter placement visit:

www.addleshawgoddard.com/graduates

THE SUNDAY TIMES
100
BEST COMPANIES
TO WORK FOR
2006

AIRBUS

www.airbus-careers.com

**Vacancies for around
70 graduates in 2007**

- Engineering
- Finance
- Human Resources
- IT
- Logistics
- Manufacturing
- Purchasing

Starting salary for 2007
£22,750

**Universities that Airbus
plans to visit in 2006-7**
Bath, Bristol, Cambridge,
London, Loughborough,
Manchester, Nottingham,
Southampton, Warwick
Please check with your university
careers service for details of events.

Application deadline
December 2006

Contact Details
Turn to page 200 now to request
more information about Airbus.

Airbus is one of the world's leading aircraft manufacturers.
As a company at the forefront of research and development
in advanced composite and metallic structures, systems
and aerodynamic design, Airbus is setting new standards
of innovation and excellence for the future.

Passion and pride among Airbus people play a major part in the drive for
success: passion about the jobs they do and pride in the product they create.
Airbus benefits from a unique workforce of over 55,000 people, which
encompasses more than 80 nationalities.

Free-thinking and entrepreneurial graduates will enjoy the chance to develop
individual talents and experience on the Airbus UK Direct Entry Graduate
Scheme (DEG). The scheme provides the opportunity to develop in-depth
knowledge of a business function through structured placements in the UK and,
potentially worldwide, with strategic partners, suppliers and customers. The
format is consistent, but specific programmes depend on the function joined,
experience, interests and current business challenges.

Airbus provides access to excellent focused training and full support to
help graduates achieve membership of professional institutions, further
qualifications and long-term career planning. Involvement in education
and community projects to broaden experience and skills in different arenas
is also actively encouraged.

There are many paths a graduate career can take as part of this pioneering
organisation. Most of the opportunities available to graduates are in design and
manufacturing engineering, with further roles in procurement, human resources,
finance, supply chain logistics, project management and information systems.

Know Airbus

Every three seconds an Airbus aircraft takes off or lands somewhere in the world.

and know how good you could be

You can build an exciting career with a global leader that continually challenges the boundaries of technology.

Airbus UK Direct Entry Graduate Scheme

ENGINEERING

MANUFACTURING

FINANCE

PROCUREMENT

INFORMATION SYSTEMS

SUPPLY CHAIN LOGISTICS

HUMAN RESOURCES

PROJECT MANAGEMENT

Airbus is one of the world's leading aircraft manufacturers and an innovative global company whose talented multi-national teams are united by one common goal: to create the future of civil aviation.

We are searching for ambitious and entrepreneurial graduates to join our specially designed Airbus UK Direct Entry Graduate Scheme.

You will need to have:
• Qualifications in Engineering or an appropriate degree
• Excellent communication and inter-personal skills
• Maximum of two years' professional experience
• Fluency in English

In return, we offer a programme of structured placements, development activities and focused training programmes in a dynamic international business environment.

Benefits of the scheme include:
• A competitive starting salary and £2,000 welcome bonus
• 25 days' paid holiday per year (plus bank holidays)
• Flexible working
• Participation in our contributory pension scheme
• Company share plan and annual profit share bonus

You will also receive wide-ranging support to gain professional qualifications and outstanding long-term prospects.

To find out more about the Airbus UK Direct Entry Graduate Scheme and details of the September 2007 intake, please visit our website:

www.airbus-careers.com

Airbus. Setting the standards.

AIRBUS

Vacancies for around
90 graduates in 2007

Retailing

Vacancies also available in Europe.

Starting salary for 2007
£38,000
Plus Audi A4

Universities that Aldi
plans to visit in 2006-7

Aston, Bath, Birmingham,
Bradford, Bristol,
Cambridge, Cardiff,
Durham, Edinburgh, Exeter,
Glasgow, Lancaster, Leeds,
Liverpool, London,
Loughborough, Manchester,
Newcastle, Nottingham,
Oxford, Reading, Sheffield,
Southampton, St Andrews,
Stirling, Surrey, Warwick,
York

Please check with your university
careers service for details of events.

Application deadline
Year-round recruitment

Contact Details
Turn to page 200 now to request
more information about Aldi.

Aldi is one of the world's largest privately owned companies and, with over 7,000 stores worldwide is recognised as a world leader in grocery retailing. Pioneers in quality discount retailing, their unique culture and philosophy promote exceptional standards of management and deliver unrivalled value for money for their customers.

The Graduate Area Management Programme offers superb opportunities for personal and career development to exceptional graduates who can prove they have drive and focus and have a record of achievement outside academia.

An individual twelve month training plan quickly introduces trainees to the pace and excitement of retail operations, trading, logistics and property management. Starting in store and managing one within weeks, the programme progresses onto multi-site responsibilities, which offer trainees the broadest opportunities to develop their leadership style, commercial awareness and technical skills. As soon as Area Management trainees are ready, they'll be given a multi-million pound area of four to six stores to run as if they owned it.

Two year secondments to Europe or the USA are a real possibility. Within five years there's every chance of a directorship reporting to the Managing Director of a region, or the Group Buying Director.

Find out more by visiting www.aldi.com and apply online. Alternatively, send a CV and a recent photograph, quoting Times 100, with a letter demonstrating your leadership potential to: Area Management Recruitment, Aldi Stores Limited, Wellington Road, South Marston Park, Swindon, Wiltshire SN3 4FN.

There's a big difference between standards and standard

Only the brightest of shining stars need apply for a place on the Aldi Graduate Area Manager Training Programme. Those 5-star, 10/10, A+ers with the motivational skills, drive and ambition to make it in the fast moving, competitive world of retailing. Naturally, you'll bring with you excellent A-level grades or equivalent and a good degree as standard. But you'll have pushed yourself in other directions too – initiating and achieving things outside the standard academic arena.

We demand these levels of excellence because they indicate the highest orders of aptitude needed to cope with the rigours of the initial training programme and onwards into your career. In just a few short weeks, you can expect to be managing a store. Then, over the following months, you'll begin to assume the responsibilities associated with Area Management – where you'll be given every opportunity to display your leadership skills and commercial awareness. When the training is over, you'll have total responsibility for four to six stores, effectively managing your own multi-million pound business.

Such levels of authority and empowerment are well beyond those you're likely to find with other employers. But then, we're not other employers. And the rewards are out of the ordinary too. The starting salary is £38K plus an Audi A4, rising in annual increments to £54½K after three years and includes a pension, private healthcare, life assurance and five weeks' holiday.

Graduate
Area Manager
Trainee
£38K + Audi A4

Area Manager
in charge of six stores
£54½K + Audi A4

Opportunity for
directorship within
5 years

There are also opportunities for Area Managers to spend two years on secondment in Europe or further afield. Within five years, there is every chance of a directorship.

Which is certainly stellar career progression by anyone's standard.

To apply, send a CV and recent photograph, together with a letter illustrating your leadership potential, quoting reference 100 to: Aldi Stores Ltd, Area Management Recruitment, Wellington Road, South Marston Park, Swindon, Wiltshire SN3 4FN. Or you can apply online at **www.aldi.com**

ALLEN & OVERY

www.allenovery.com/careeruk

Vacancies for around
120 graduates in 2007
For training contracts starting in 2009

 Law

Starting salary for 2007
£31,000

Universities Allen & Overy plans to visit in 2006-7
Bath, Birmingham, Bristol, Cambridge, Cardiff, City, Dublin, Durham, East Anglia, Edinburgh, Essex, Exeter, Leeds, Leicester, London, Manchester, Newcastle, Northumbria, Nottingham, Oxford, Oxford Brookes, Reading, Sheffield, Southampton, St Andrews, Warwick, York
Please check with your university careers service for details of events.

Application deadline
See website for full details.

Contact Details
✉ graduate.recruitment
@allenovery.com
☎ 020 7330 3000
Turn to page 200 now to request more information about Allen & Overy.

Allen & Overy is an international legal practice with 4,800 people in 25 major centres worldwide. The practice's client list includes many of the world's top businesses, financial institutions, governments and private individuals.

Allen & Overy is renowned for the high quality of its banking, international capital markets and corporate advice but also has major strengths in litigation, employment pensions and incentives, tax, real estate and private client. Within this broad range of expertise the practice offers a training contract characterized by flexibility and choice. Allen & Overy's training programme is widely regarded as the best in the City and continues throughout a career with the practice.

Vital to their success is the way they approach their work. Allen & Overy people enjoy what they do and want to employ people who think the same way, maintaining a professional, supportive and friendly working environment.

Allen & Overy recruits 120 trainee solicitors each year and welcome applications from both law and non-law candidates. At least an upper second-class degree is expected.

Given the strength of the practice's international corporate, banking and ICM departments, trainees spend 12 months working in these areas. They also gain contentious experience in either litigation or employment. In addition, there are also opportunities for trainees to undertake international and client secondments. By working closely with their trainers and other colleagues, trainees develop practical experience and enjoy a high level of early responsibility.

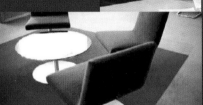

▲ Arcadia Group Limited

Vacancies for around 200-250 graduates in 2007

- Accountancy
- Finance
- General Management
- Human Resources
- Purchasing
- Retailing

Starting salary for 2007
£17,000-£22,500

Universities that Arcadia Group plans to visit in 2006-7
Edinburgh, Glasgow, Leicester, London, Manchester, Northumbria, Nottingham Trent, Oxford Brookes, Strathclyde
Please check with your university careers service for details of events.

Application deadline
Year-round recruitment

Contact Details
Turn to page 200 now to request more information about Arcadia Group.

The Arcadia Group is one of the UK's largest fashion retail companies with over 25,000 employees, 2,000 outlets throughout the UK and a growing number of international stores. The group includes eight celebrated high street brands – Burton, Dorothy Perkins, Evans, Outfit, Miss Selfridge, Topshop, Topman and Wallis.

Arcadia offer careers that appeal to a diverse range of individuals – from those of you with a strong numerical background to fashion fanatics with an eye for trends. Fast track Graduate opportunities exist in retail management, merchandising, distribution, buying, human resources and finance.

Arcadia are renowned for their commitment to the training and personal development of graduates. Development opportunities include specially designed programmes, formal courses, support for professional qualifications and competency based training. Structured personal development plans enable graduates to develop their portfolio of skills and recognise their potential. With outstanding drive and commitment graduates can achieve promotion at the earliest opportunity.

Enthusiasm, commerciality and customer focus in addition to a love of fashion are the qualities that will ensure a successful career at Arcadia. In return, graduates will be given early responsibility, structured training and development and the opportunity to make an impact on the most forward thinking fashion retail business in the UK.

To find out all about what Arcadia have to offer visit:
www.arcadiagroup.co.uk/recruitment

YOUR FUTURE
in fashion

The Arcadia Group is one of the largest fashion retailers in the UK, boasting the most exciting, innovative brands on the high street today — Burton, Dorothy Perkins, Evans, Outfit, Miss Selfridge, Topshop, Topman and Wallis. Continuing to expand internationally, our business is bold, our brands market-leading and our career opportunities endless.

Award winning and acclaimed as a graduate recruiter, Arcadia offer a diverse range of opportunities, whether you are looking for a career at the sharp end of the business or behind the scenes.

Arcadia are currently recruiting Graduates into the following careers:

- Retail Management
- Merchandising
- Distribution
- Buying
- Human Resources
- Finance

If you want to make an impact on the most forward thinking fashion retail business in the UK, apply online today:

www.arcadiagroup.co.uk/recruitment

ARMY
BE THE BEST

Vacancies for around
1,000 **graduates in 2007**

- Accountancy
- Engineering
- Finance
- General Management
- Human Resources
- IT
- Law
- Logistics
- Marketing
- Research & Development

Vacancies also available throughout the world.

Starting salary for 2007
£27,068

Universities the Army plans to visit in 2006-7
Please check with your university careers service for details of events.

Application deadline
Year-round recruitment

Contact Details
☎ 08457 300 111
Turn to page 200 now to request more information about the Army.

Being an Army officer is unlike any other job – from leading a platoon of 30 soldiers one week to organising a team on adventurous training the next. The Army engages with graduates and trains them to become some of the best leaders in the world.

As one of the most respected and technologically advanced organisations in the world, the Army can offer unrivalled training and development to graduates of all disciplines, enhancing management and leadership potential and providing the skills and self-confidence to excel in the Army and, later on, in civilian careers.

Beyond the many career-enhancing qualities graduates will pick up, there are many personal rewards for most officers – they will find it incredibly satisfying to discover what they're capable of under different kinds of pressure. After just one year, officers can be responsible for over 30 soldiers and several million pounds worth of equipment.

Graduates start their officer training at the Royal Military Academy Sandhurst (RMAS) where they learn all aspects of soldiering, management and leadership training. On completion, they will join their Regiment or Corps where they will undergo specialist training for their chosen job. Subsequently, officers may study for Army-sponsored or vocational qualifications.

If the career development isn't enough to tempt them, perhaps some of the other aspects of being an officer will – the Army provides a challenging career, continuous professional development, great promotional prospects, unrivalled travel and sporting opportunities and an excellent remuneration and benefits package.

LEAD FROM THE FRONT

Being an Army officer is unlike any other job. One week you can be making tough decisions in unfamiliar territory, under pressure and leading a platoon of 30 soldiers, and then the next week organising a team on adventurous training. The Army engages with graduates from all disciplines and trains them to become some of the best leaders in the world and with a starting salary of £27,068 upon completion of training, a job as an Army officer pays in more ways than one.

Captain Dominic Smith's interest in the Army began at university and since then he has travelled the world, pursued sporting passions and gained two civilian qualifications.

"I joined the Officer Training Corps at university as it allowed me to spend weekends adventurous training, enjoying a great social life and taking part in new sports. During that time, I received a salary, learnt new skills and developed an appetite for skiing. I realised an Army career was too great an opportunity to ignore."

"I applied the training I received at Sandhurst as a Troop Commander on Operation Telic in Iraq, taking responsibility for 11 soldiers and three Challenger tanks. Shortly after returning, I spent two weeks sailing around the Baltic Sea with the same soldiers."

If you've always had the ability to understand what needs to be done in a high pressure situation and can communicate it clearly, then chances are you'll be more suited than you think to a career as an Army officer.

To find out more about leading from the front, visit: **www.armyofficer.mod.uk** or contact **08457 300 111**.

ARMY
BE THE BEST

TERRITORIAL ARMY
BE THE BEST

ASDA

Vacancies for around 80 graduates in 2007

- ◼ Finance
- ◼ General Management
- ◼ Human Resources
- ◼ IT
- ◼ Logistics
- ◼ Purchasing
- ◼ Retailing

Starting salary for 2007
£21,500

Universities that ASDA plans to visit in 2006-7
Leeds, Manchester, Newcastle, Northumbria, Nottingham Trent
Please check with your university careers service for details of events.

Application deadline
Year-round recruitment

Contact Details
Turn to page 200 now to request more information about ASDA.

Voted the UK's best place to work by the Financial Times and named one of Europe's best employers by Fortune magazine, ASDA is one of the UK's fastest-growing retailers. With over 13 million customers per week, 163,000 employees and more than 300 stores, ASDA's success is down to attitude: the fact that each and every person who works there is proud to be part of the team – and keen to join in wherever they're needed.

Naturally, ASDA are looking for people with the potential to manage their multi-million pound stores. But that's not all. They also have exciting opportunities in a variety of areas like Logistics, Trading, Finance, IT, Construction and Property, HR and George. Each business function has its own specific training and development opportunities, but wherever successful applicants join, they'll be given real responsibility from an early stage and will have a Buddy who can help them with issues they may have.

The kinds of people who impress ASDA are down-to-earth – egos are a big no-no. They like outgoing, enthusiastic types who are courteous to everyone they meet. They consider degrees in all disciplines, and are especially interested in extra-curricular experience like industrial placements or a year out.

On top of the salary, graduates will have a bonus scheme, discount card, pension, healthcare, life assurance, share plans and 24 days' holiday. Graduates will also enjoy uncompromising support for their development, with the aim of placing them in a middle-management role after three years and senior management after five.

AstraZeneca

www.ideas.astrazeneca.com

Vacancies for around 25-30 graduates in 2007

- Engineering
- Finance
- IT
- Logistics
- Marketing
- Purchasing
- Research & Development

I want to be recognised

Starting salary for 2007
£25,000-£28,000

Universities AstraZeneca plans to visit in 2006-7
Please check with your university careers service for details of events.

Application deadline
Year-round recruitment
See website for full details.

Contact Details
Turn to page 200 now to request more information about AstraZeneca.

One of the world's leading pharmaceutical companies, AstraZeneca turns great ideas into innovative medicines which make real difference to peoples lives.

The company's excellent reputation and diversity of graduate opportunities make them the natural choice for candidates from a science background. However, their strengths in manufacturing and commerce mean they can also provide challenges to graduates from other disciplines. Whatever their degree subject, graduates will be excited by the quality and diversity of opportunity. Programmes are designed to progress careers through an integrated range of flexible training activities and blended learning ideas.

From day-one induction and personal mentoring to management and global leadership programmes, AstraZeneca provides the resources and support graduates need to reach their full potential; while cross-functional moves, secondments and international assignments can broaden the experience. It is a performance-based culture with competitive salaries and bonuses that are linked to overall progress. But they also believe that quality of life and quality of work go hand in hand. That's why they actively pursue opportunities for flexible working arrangements.

Core benefits include a minimum level of pension contribution and healthcare provision, and the additional range of 'rewards options' is considerable. But these are benefits that people tend to appreciate further down the line. What probably excites graduates more at this stage is the opportunity to develop their skills within a truly global business that's setting the standards in an industry rich in challenges and rewards.

I want to go further

Graduate opportunities, all disciplines.

It's only possible to achieve your full potential when you're given the proper support and resources. At AstraZeneca, we're committed to our graduates' success and reward people on the basis of performance.

take your ambitions forward at
ideas.astrazeneca.com
sign up for job alerts and let the opportunities come to you

AstraZeneca
life inspiring ideas

ATKINS

Vacancies for around
250 **graduates in 2007**

- Consulting
- Engineering

Vacancies also available elsewhere
in the world.

Starting salary for 2007
£Competitive

**Universities that Atkins
plans to visit in 2006-7**
Bath, Belfast, Birmingham,
Bristol, Cambridge, Cardiff,
Heriot-Watt, Leeds,
Liverpool, London,
Loughborough, Manchester,
Newcastle, Nottingham,
Oxford, Sheffield,
Southampton, Surrey,
Swansea
Please check with your university
careers service for details of events.

Application deadline
Year-round recruitment

Contact Details
✉ graduates@atkinsglobal.com
☎ 0121 483 5553
Turn to page 200 now to request
more information about Atkins.

Atkins is a leading provider of professional, technology-based consultancy and support services, and a major player in a diversity of sectors. These include building design, highways, rail, aviation, water, oil and gas, power, nuclear, defence and the environment.

As a multi-disciplinary consultant, Atkins plays a key role in many high-profile projects. The company is designing the stunning Regatta hotel and apartment complex in Jakarta; supporting Airbus in the development of the world's largest airliner, the A380; and managing 23% of UK highways. Atkins also helped transform Trafalgar Square from a congested traffic blackspot into a vibrant public space.

With such a breadth and depth of capabilities, Atkins offers unparalleled opportunities to build a rewarding career. With Atkins, graduates can work with 15,000 of the brightest people in the industry in 125+ offices around the world, using analytical skills developed at university to learn new problem-solving techniques. Atkins provides continuing professional development through accredited training, set out by professional institutes, plus personal development events.

A company that's as committed to diversity as it is to excellence, Atkins welcomes graduates from the following disciplines: engineering – aerospace, building services, chemical, civil, electrical/electronic, geotechnical, mechanical, structural; architecture; environmental; maths/physics; planning (transport & urban); software development/computer science; surveying (building & quantity); and transport systems. Specific vacancies are given on Atkins' website.

BAE SYSTEMS

Vacancies for around
200 graduates in 2007

- Engineering
- Finance
- General Management
- Human Resources
- Logistics
- Marketing
- Purchasing
- Research & Development
- Sales

Starting salary for 2007
£22,000-£26,000

Universities BAE Systems plans to visit in 2006-7
Bath, Bristol, Cardiff, Edinburgh, Glasgow, Heriot-Watt, Lancaster, Leeds, Leicester, Loughborough, Manchester, Newcastle, Nottingham, Nottingham Trent, Sheffield, Southampton, Strathclyde, Warwick
Please check with your university careers service for details of events.

Application deadline
31st December 2006

Contact Details
☎ 01772 677277
Turn to page 200 now to request more information about BAE Systems.

In the exciting arena of international defence, BAE Systems is a leading player with a wealth of opportunities for both undergraduates and graduates. Their business extends globally with a range of programmes in the land, sea and air sectors.

The company recognises that no two people are alike and aim to offer a range of career paths that appeal to a broad range of individuals. They have three graduate entry programmes; 'GDF' is the main programme, 'FLDP' for those looking for a finance leadership career and 'SIGMA' for fast-track international leadership.

'GDF' is the graduate programme that offers training and development alongside on-the-job development. Graduates can use the opportunities of the GDF to develop their own networks across the UK business.

BAE Systems have a large requirement for engineers; in particular, manufacturing & production, mechanical, electrical, systems, software, project management, microwave and quality. On the business side, they are looking for commercial, procurement, project management, sales & marketing and human resources.

Graduates are supported by their line manager and corporate mentor. Where appropriate they will also be supported in gaining chartership. The full package offered by BAE Systems includes a competitive salary (£22,000 to £26,000) with six-monthly performance reviews, an initial sign-up payment of £2,000, 25 days holiday per year and a number of discounted healthcare, car lease and share schemes.

BAKER & McKENZIE

**Vacancies for around
38 graduates in 2007**
For training contracts starting in 2009

■ Law

Starting salary in 2006
£31,500

**Universities that
Baker & McKenzie
plans to visit in 2006-7**
Birmingham, Bristol,
Cambridge, Durham, Exeter,
Leeds, London, Manchester,
Nottingham, Oxford,
Warwick
Please check with your university
careers service for details of events.

Application deadline
See website for full details.

Contact Details
✉ london.graduate.recruit
@bakernet.com
☎ 020 7919 1000
Turn to page 200 now to request more
information about Baker & McKenzie.

Baker & McKenzie in London offers unparalleled opportunities to become a first class lawyer in the world's largest global law firm. With a network covering 70 locations in 38 countries and a presence in virtually every important financial and commercial centre worldwide, the firm is able to attract the highest quality multi-jurisdictional clients.

Baker & McKenzie look for graduates who are stimulated by intellectual challenge and want to be 'the best' at what they do. Effective communication together with the ability to be creative but practical problem solvers, team players and a sense of humour are qualities which will help candidates stand out from the crowd. In return, the firm provides exceptional training – a commitment which won them 'Best Trainer – Large City Firm' at the 2006 LCN-TSG Training and Recruitment Awards for the third consecutive year.

The two year training programme commences with an interactive and practical induction focusing on key skills – problem solving, interviewing, presenting and IT. There are four six-month 'seats' which include one in the corporate department and one contentious. Trainees are given early responsibility on high profile transactions and the opportunity to go on client or international secondments to such places as Sydney, Chicago, Moscow, Hong Kong and Tokyo.

Baker & McKenzie's commitment to training begins even before starting a career with the firm through the London and International Summer Placements.

BARCLAYS

www.barclays-graduates.com

Vacancies for around 100 graduates in 2007

- Accountancy
- Finance
- General Management
- Human Resources
- IT
- Marketing
- Retailing
- Sales

Vacancies also available in Europe, Asia and elsewhere in the world.

Starting salary for 2007

£24,000

Plus £3,500 joining bonus and £3,550 travel allowance.

Universities Barclays Bank plans to visit in 2006-7

Bath, Birmingham, Bristol, Cambridge, Dublin, Durham, Edinburgh, Loughborough, Manchester, Nottingham, Oxford, Warwick
Please check with your university careers service for details of events.

Application deadline

31st December 2006

Contact Details

✉ barclays.graduates@reed.co.uk

Turn to page 200 now to request more information about Barclays Bank.

Throughout their history, Barclays' reputation has been built on a spirit of innovation. They were the first bank to install a computer, the first to issue credit cards and the first to launch ATMs. It's this fresh thinking approach that makes Barclays such an inspiring place for graduates to develop their career.

Barclays have opportunities in Business Banking, Retail Banking, Global Retail and Commercial Banking, Barclaycard, Finance, Treasury, Information Technology, Chief Administration Office, Marketing and Human Resources.

Each business area has a graduate programme lasting between one and three years. It's up to graduates to decide which area best suits them – visit Barclays' website for information on each programme.

Barclays are looking for ambitious graduates who know where they want to be – and have the drive and initiative to get there. Graduates will have responsibility from the outset, so they need to be committed to pushing their own abilities and making a real impact on the business as a whole. A strong academic background is important but there's more to it than that and extra-curricular experience like summer placements and gap years are also extremely relevant.

A mixture of formal training and on-the-job learning will equip graduates with the skills and experience they need to be successful at Barclays. Successful applicants will have opportunities to gain a professional qualification and up to £2,000 to spend on their personal development in line with their chosen role. And their development doesn't stop at the end of the programme. Career-long learning is a priority at Barclays: this is just the beginning.

The world's first ATM.

Inspired by a long queue and a short lunch hour.

Graduate Careers 2007

Inspired by Barclays

Business Banking | Retail Banking | International Retail & Commercial Banking | Treasury | Finance | Marketing | HR | IT | Barclaycard

Whether we're shaking up the world of banking with ground-breaking ideas like this one, or coming up with new and exciting ways to support the communities we serve, there's a spirit of innovation at Barclays that sets us apart in the financial services sector. For ambitious graduates like you, it's this refusal to accept the established ways of working that makes Barclays such an inspiring place to develop a career. Find out more at **www.inspiredbybarclays.com**

 We'll judge you on your ability and nothing else.

BARCLAYS CAPITAL

Vacancies for around
400 graduates in 2007

■ Finance

▨ Investment Banking

■ IT

Vacancies also available in
Europe and Asia.

Be individual. Take charge. Expect challenge.

Starting salary for 2007
£Competitive

Universities that
Barclays Capital
plans to visit in 2006-7

Bristol, Cambridge,
Dublin, Durham, Edinburgh,
London, Manchester,
Nottingham, Oxford,
Warwick

Please check with your university
careers service for details of events.

Application deadline
30th November 2006
Early application advised.

Contact Details

Turn to page 200 now to request more
information about Barclays Capital.

Barclays Capital is the investment banking division of Barclays Bank PLC which has an AA long-term credit rating and a balance sheet of over £924 billion.

With a distinctive business model, Barclays Capital provides large corporate, government and institutional clients with solutions to their financing and risk management needs. Barclays Capital has offices in 26 countries, employs over 9,000 people and has the global reach and distribution power to meet the needs of issuers and investors worldwide.

Barclays Capital's graduate programme is key to their success and is supported by senior management throughout the organisation. On the programme, graduates are provided with an excellent understanding of financial markets, as well as the firm's products, instruments and services. This creates a strong platform on which to build more specialist expertise. The programme takes learning one step further, incorporating practical applications through a variety of case studies, workshops and presentations.

Depending on the area joined, each graduate receives comprehensive, role-specific training as well as training in soft skills. Barclays Capital also encourages people to obtain appropriate professional qualifications. And that's just the beginning.

Visit their website for more information on the careers they offer.
www.barclayscapital.com/campusrecruitment

Think about Barclays Capital.

Graduates – Investment Banking

Think about everything you want from a career, and then ask who can make you the perfect offer. Decide whether you want to work for another firm, or for a firm where we actually do believe that our graduates are the future.

With the support of a parent bank with a balance sheet of over £924 billion, we have offices in 26 countries employing over 9,000 people.

Only eight years old, we are expanding every year. So yes, we are a world leading investment bank, but we are also a meritocracy where the individual is valued, but the team is paramount. We truly believe we are different.

So, if you have an outstanding undergraduate or master's degree, visit our website for more information.

www.barclayscapital.com/campusrecruitment

BBC

www.bbc.co.uk/jobs

Possible Vacancies in 2007

- Accountancy
- Engineering
- Finance
- Law
- Marketing
- Media
- Research & Development

Starting salary for 2007
£Competitive

Universities that the BBC plans to visit in 2006-7
Please check with your university careers service for details of events.

Application deadline
Year-round recruitment

Contact Details
✉ recruitment@bbc.co.uk
☎ 0870 333 1330
Turn to page 200 now to request more information about the BBC.

The BBC aims to be the most creative and trusted broadcaster and programme maker in the world, seeking to satisfy all its audiences worldwide with television, radio and internet services that inform, educate and entertain. In terms of recruitment, it aims to attract an increasingly diverse workforce representative of the population it serves.

The environment new joiners find themselves working in is friendly, welcoming and open to change. Hours are variable and dress code relaxed – it couldn't be further removed from the standard nine-to-five.

Opportunities arise in a wide range of roles. These include journalism, programme making, administration and technical areas. What all areas look for is enthusiasm, motivation and relevant experience, though not necessarily through paid previous employment.

Although intermittently there are advertised training schemes, most graduates tend to enter the BBC through one-off vacancies advertised throughout the year, rarely if ever mentioning possession of a degree as a pre-requisite.

The common denominator for people working at the BBC, regardless of their particular role and where they work in the organisation is a genuine passion for the work they do. The reward for such commitment is the BBC's keen attention to staff development.

People are encouraged to give serious thought to their career planning and training needs, and an attachment system gives staff the opportunity to gain experience in other areas of work.

AS FAR AS YOU'LL GET FROM THE STANDARD 9 TO 5

WHAT DID YOU EXPECT?

Sharing your talent with the BBC is one of the most fulfilling and exciting decisions you can make. After all, you'd be joining an organisation whose consistent innovation and creativity continues to challenge accepted boundaries and win awards around the world. Whatever role you play, you'll apply your imagination and passion to ensuring that we continue to entertain, educate and inform our many diverse audiences.

Everyone wants to find an inspirational place where they'll be encouraged to do things differently. You just have. Visit **bbc.co.uk/jobs** to find out more about the roles available and what it takes to succeed here.

Bloomberg

careers.bloomberg.com

Vacancies for around 600 graduates in 2007

- Finance
- IT
- Media
- Research & Development
- Sales

Vacancies also available
in Europe and Asia.

Starting salary for 2007
£Competitive

Universities that Bloomberg plans to visit in 2006-7
Please check with your university careers service for details of events.

Application deadline
Year-round recruitment

Contact Details
✉ bethebest@bloomberg.net

Turn to page 200 now to request more information about Bloomberg.

Bloomberg is the leading global provider of data, news and analytics. The Bloomberg Terminal and Bloomberg's media services provide real-time and archived financial and market data, pricing, trading, news and communications tools in a single, integrated package.

Bloomberg's clients include corporations, news organisations, financial and legal professionals and individuals around the world. With 8,000 employees operating in 127 countries, Bloomberg is truly international. The largest offices include New York, London and Tokyo and this is where the majority of graduate opportunities are located.

Graduate positions include financial sales, programming, global data, customer support, IT, project management and many more. For most roles a second language is desirable but not essential. Bloomberg recruit all year round and from any discipline. A passion for finance, programming, media or languages is required. Bloomberg breaks down barriers between people and encourages communication by bringing colleagues together. With no job titles or executive areas, the culture fosters interaction at every level.

Bloomberg support community programmes by reinvesting resources back into society through sponsorships and employee volunteer activities. But the real depth and diversity of Bloomberg's way of life comes from the creativity and commitment of its people. Training is extensive and ongoing via Bloomberg University. Courses are wide-ranging and available to all, allowing graduates to progress quickly and take on real responsibility fast. Opportunities are all listed on the website and start dates are available throughout the year.

bp

www.bp.com/careers

Vacancies for around
100 **graduates in 2007**

- Engineering
- Finance
- IT
- Research & Development

Vacancies also available in Europe.

Starting salary for 2007
£28,000

Universities that BP plans to visit in 2006-7
Please check with your university careers service for details of events.

Application deadline
Year-round recruitment

Contact Details
Turn to page 200 now to request more information about BP.

As winner of the 'Graduate Employer of the Year' at the 2005 Target Awards and short listed for the 'Graduate Employer of the Year' at the 2006 Target Awards, BP's graduate programmes offer an exciting career with a global blue-chip company from day one.

With the chance to experience varied and challenging placements either at home or, in some cases, further afield, graduates will discover unique opportunities in vibrant, energetic areas such as: marketing, procurement, operations, trading, finance, business analysis, digital business, project evaluation and mergers and acquisitions.

Of course, technical graduates can gain cutting-edge technology experience in positions focused on geoscience, and many areas of engineering including: chemical, instrument, control and electrical, mechanical, petroleum and drilling. For applicants who are excited by technology and who look for improvements at every turn, BP might be the right choice.

Wherever the position, graduates will be supported and encouraged to exceed both personal and professional targets by mentors and colleagues alike.

BP values drive, enthusiasm, ambition and the ability to think creatively and work well with others and are looking for people willing to learn and ready to make a difference. Those entering technical roles will need to show an acute understanding of their discipline.

BP recognises that at the core of its success, are its people. By joining BP, graduates will gain the kind of comprehensive training, support and progression expected from a world-leading organisation, coupled with a wide range of other associated benefits.

Put simply, this is an industry in which your contribution can have a huge impact. The issue of energy is one that's crucial to everybody's future. So when I was looking for a career I was impressed by BP's commitment to being a force for good.
I couldn't think of a better place to use my talents.

Graduate careers

BP offers graduates an amazing breadth of opportunity and experience. We face enormous challenges for the future – but fantastic opportunities too. To help us, we need committed and talented people: people who will in time become the scientists and engineers, finance and business professionals who will lead us in the future. That's why we invest so much in you today. We seek the best and the brightest from all over the world, and when we find you we make sure you are supported, stimulated and challenged.

As well as on-job learning, structured courses and personal study, you'll build an international network of expert friends and talented colleagues. You'll find a wealth of memorable experiences in each of the three different placements you take on. And you'll earn more than a generous salary – you'll be earning valuable professional qualifications too.

To find out more and to apply, please visit www.bp.com/careers

We open for applications from September 2006.

For information on our company, please visit www.bp.com

BP is an equal opportunities employer

bp

beyond petroleum

www.bt.com/grads

Vacancies for around
200-250 **graduates in 2007**

- Consulting
- Engineering
- Finance
- General Management
- Human Resources
- IT
- Marketing
- Purchasing
- Research & Development
- Sales

Vacancies also available in Europe.

Starting salary for 2007
£Competitive

Universities that BT plans to visit in 2006-7
Aston, Bath, Belfast, Birmingham, Cambridge, Cardiff, Durham, Edinburgh, Lancaster, Leeds, Loughborough, Manchester, Newcastle, Nottingham, Oxford, Sheffield, Southampton, Ulster, Warwick
Please check with your university careers service for details of events.

Application deadline
See website for full details.

Contact Details
Turn to page 200 now to request more information about BT.

Change = different things to different people.

The market is changing. Technology is changing. BT's changing. Be part of a team that is transforming the way businesses communicate in nearly 200 countries around the world across five continents.

BT is more than being well known for telecommunications and IT solutions. BT provides ground-breaking solutions and works with well-known and global companies; significantly changing the way they operate. To achieve this, BT has the most inspiring people in the industry; managing projects, pushing the boundaries and delivering the most advanced and innovative solutions to date.

Four development streams are on offer: Professional Services, ICT & Research, Functionalist Specialists and Customer Interface. Customer service, finance, human resources, marketing, procurement and sales, ICT, engineering, research and development are just some of the roles that graduates are placed in.

At least a 2.1 Honours Degree or international equivalent particularly in computer science, business-related subjects, general science or engineering is required as well as GCSE (or equivalent qualification) in mathematics and English at Grade C (Grade B mathematics for the finance programme). A permanent right to work in the UK is a pre-requisite and language skills would be a big asset. BT is looking for their leaders of the future so the ability to demonstrate strong leadership potential, to really stand out from the crowd, is required.

A two-year fast-paced core graduate development scheme with responsibility on real projects from day one is offered, with support and coaching from line managers, as well as unlimited prospects for advancement for high achievers.

BT is an equal opportunities employer.

Change =

To some, change brings uncertainty.
To us, it brings energy, freshness and opportunities.

At BT we're in the business of change. BT's evolving all the
time. Our work is driving change in broader society and we're
revolutionising the way businesses communicate. To achieve
our goals, we're bringing together a new breed of people.
Individuals who have the attributes required to thrive and
relish the challenge of a change environment.

If you feel you have what it takes and thrive
on challenges, we'd love to hear from you.

Visit www.bt.com/grads.

Bringing it all together

INVESTOR IN PEOPLE

BT is an equal
opportunity
employer

Cadbury Schweppes

Vacancies for around 25 graduates in 2007

- Accountancy
- Engineering
- Finance
- Human Resources
- IT
- Logistics
- Manufacturing
- Marketing
- Research & Development
- Sales

Starting salary in 2006
£24,000

Universities that Cadbury Schweppes plans to visit in 2006-7

Bath, Birmingham, Bristol, Cambridge, Cardiff, Edinburgh, Nottingham, Oxford, Sheffield, Warwick

Please check with your university careers service for details of events.

Application deadline
See website for full details.

Contact Details

✉ csgraduates@csplc.com

Turn to page 200 now to request more information about Cadbury Schweppes.

With global strength unrivalled by even the hugest tube of Extra Strong Mints and an unstoppable future-focused ambition, every one of Cadbury Schweppes' 50,000-strong global family comes together to create far more than just chocolate.

Be it accountancy or engineering, manufacturing or marketing, people, products or pear drops – a career in any one of Cadbury Schweppes' six major global functions offers something far from the ordinary.

Naturally, graduates will get all of the responsibility and top drawer experiences they could wish for from the start. It goes without saying that they'll get global opportunities aplenty, with a whole world of confectionery projects to keep track of. And with bags of opportunity for graduates to work their magic with mammoth brands; build an interesting, enviable career; sculpt some terrific travel experiences and boost their prospects with tailor-made training – the only possible thing left to ask for would be a friendly, supportive environment in which to become a true business leader of the future – and of course they'll get that too.

Those with talent, tenacity and a spark that sets them apart will have exactly what Cadbury Schweppes demands: the drive and motivation to become the living, breathing future of a world-class player. Not only that, what graduates get in return is pretty incalculable. Aside from the competitive salary and great benefits, add a diverse community of like-minded peers and support in getting relevant professional qualifications, and Cadbury Schweppes' graduates will be set for success on a truly amazing scale.

Go to www.cadburyschweppes.com/ukgraduates

big business with a rather tasty twist

CANCER RESEARCH UK

jobs.cancerresearchuk.org

Vacancies for around
50 graduates in 2007

◼ **Marketing**

◼ **Research & Development**

Starting salary for 2007
Competitive

Universities that
Cancer Research UK
plans to visit in 2006-7
Please check with your university
careers service for details of events.

Application deadline
See website for details.

Contact Details
Turn to page 200 now to request more
information about Cancer Research UK.

Cancer Research UK is the world's leading independent organisation dedicated to cancer research. Over 3,000 of the world's best doctors, nurses and scientific staff work on their pioneering research. But equally important are the dedicated individuals in fundraising, marketing, HR, communications, IT, finance and other support functions.

Last year, their income topped £420 million – an achievement that underlines the business expertise, commercial vision and marketing talent that supports the groundbreaking research work at their world-class centre of scientific excellence. So wherever graduates join them they can expect to make a real contribution from day one. And to help successful applicants achieve their own ambitions, they will benefit from a unique combination of on-the-job learning and formal, professional training.

Clearly, a career with Cancer Research UK offers plenty in the way of personal fulfilment. But what many people overlook is how commercially challenging and professionally rewarding their work can be. So while empathy for the cause is important, above all they're looking for ambitious, business-minded graduates who can help drive the organisation forward in the months and years to come.

Every year, Cancer Research UK offers a variety of graduate opportunities in all aspects of their work, including fundraising, science and corporate support services. To find out more about specific opportunities, visit their website. Graduates can also sign up for email alerts which will keep them up to date with any relevant vacancies at http://jobs.cancerresearchuk.org/alerts_signup_form.php

NOBODY UNDERSTANDS QUITE LIKE JAMES THE DIFFERENCE YOU CAN MAKE.

James was six when he was diagnosed with Acute Lymphoblastic Leukaemia. 18 months on, and midway through an intensive course of treatment, his outlook is getting brighter by the day. James is just one of more than 100,000 people with cancer who, thanks to our groundbreaking work, are treated successfully each year. To ensure we keep furthering our knowledge, we're looking for talented graduates to join us across the organisation. These are top-flight opportunities for top-flight graduates. Which is why we're looking for individuals who not only empathise with the work we do, but have the talent, ambition and commercial nous to push us on to even greater things. Ready to make a difference? Then find out more at www.cancerresearchuk.org/aboutus/jobs

Registered charity no. 1089464

CANCER RESEARCH UK

citigroup

www.citigroup.com

Vacancies for around 200 **graduates in 2007**

- Human Resources
- Investment Banking
- IT

Vacancies also available throughout the world.

Starting salary for 2007
£Competitive

Universities Citigroup plans to visit in 2006-7
Please check with your university careers service for details of events.

Application deadline
6th November 2006

Contact Details
Turn to page 200 now to request more information about Citigroup.

Citigroup's goal is to be the most respected global financial services company. No financial institution is more committed to understanding and advancing the financial objectives of its clients.

Citigroup Corporate and Investment Banking has become a market leader, expertly serving the needs of corporations, governments and institutions with a broad range of financial products and services. From stock brokerage to research analysis, investment banking to global transaction services, Citigroup provides more industry-leading solutions to more clients in more countries than any of its competitors.

This is a world-class firm that actively seeks to recruit the best. Working at Citigroup means embracing stimulating and challenging work, being at the centre of the financial industry, and having the chance to have a truly global career. It demands candidates who will thrive in this environment, who have an excellent academic background, the ability to work independently as well as in teams, and perform under pressure. In return Citigroup offer analysts and interns excellent training, a wealth of opportunities and competitive financial rewards.

People who join Citigroup benefit from a rigorous and structured development programme, which is reinforced through on-the-job training and further development opportunities. Ongoing training and development is something that is encouraged and supported throughout the firm.

Citigroup believes in providing outstanding people with the best opportunity to realise their potential, and recruits into a broad range of business areas and from all degree disciplines.

"I found myself sharing thoughts from day one with the most respected professionals in the industry, who originated some of the deals on the FT covers that we read back in university. For me that was quite impressive."

ENRIQUE BECERRA, ASSOCIATE
INVESTMENT BANKING

Global Banking
- Investment Banking
- Corporate Banking

Global Capital Markets
- Capital Markets Origination
- Equity Sales & Trading
- Fixed Income Sales & Trading

Global Transaction Services

Citigroup Investment Research

Global Corporate Services
- Technology
- Operations
- Human Resources

Working at Citigroup means being part of a team that is making history in the financial services world. If this appeals to you, come see us. We're looking forward to meeting you.

apply online at **www.oncampus.citigroup.com**

CIVIL SERVICE FASTSTREAM

Vacancies for around 300 graduates in 2007

- General Management
- IT

Starting salary for 2007
£23,800

Universities the
Fast Stream
plans to visit in 2006-7
Aberdeen, Aberystwyth,
Bangor, Bath, Birmingham,
Bristol, Essex, London,
Newcastle, Sheffield
Please check with your university
careers service for details of events.

Application deadline
30th November 2006

Contact Details
✉ faststream@parity.net
☎ 01276 400333
Turn to page 200 now to request
more information about Fast Stream.

When reading the headlines, who actually deals with the issues they raise? Who decides on controls for avian flu; on security provision for the 2012 Olympic Games? Who delivers a step-change in services to the public? Who represents the UK on the world scene? The Civil Service.

The Civil Service Fast Stream is a training and development programme for graduates with the potential to reach the top. Fast Streamers are groomed for senior management positions. From the outset, graduates move regularly between projects to acquire a range of business skills. They'll also be given considerable responsibility early on. Later, graduates will focus on one of three career groups: corporate services, operational delivery or policy delivery – but to reach the top they'll need experience in more than one area.

The Fast Stream is no easy option. Graduates need to be thorough, articulate and persuasive with a minimum 2:2 in any discipline and an intelligent, analytical and open-minded approach. Above all, they'll need to be the kind of person who gets results, able to deliver high-quality services to the public.

The training programme is exemplary and tailored to meet individual needs, combining on-the-job training and formal courses. Regardless of gender, ethnic origin, disability, sexuality or marital status, the Fast Stream looks forward to applications from people who have what it takes to make a difference.

The Fast Stream offers many opportunities but there are plenty more across the Civil Service. Visit www.careers.civil-service.gov.uk to see other opportunities that are available.

**MONITORING THE MIGRATION OF BIRDS IS
ONE WAY OF CONTROLLING AVIAN FLU.**

BE WHERE IT MATTERS

**BUT IS THIS ENOUGH? ARE VACCINE STOCKS
SUFFICIENT? ARE FARMERS PROTECTED?**

Imagine being at the heart of the most important issues around. Delivering initiatives, implementing them and providing vital corporate support. This is the life of a Civil Service Fast Streamer. Our dedicated training and development will expose you to all sorts of challenges, while giving you the skills to advance. Gender, sexual orientation, race and disability are irrelevant – we're more interested in your ability, outlook and intellectual capability. If you want to shape the future by joining the Fast Stream, visit www.faststream.gov.uk or call 01276 400333.

CLIFFORD CHANCE

Vacancies for around
130 **graduates in 2007**
For training contracts starting in 2009

■ Law

Starting salary for 2007
£31,000

**Universities that
Clifford Chance
plans to visit in 2006-7**
Belfast, Bristol, Cambridge,
Durham, Edinburgh, Exeter,
Leeds, London, Manchester,
Nottingham, Oxford,
Sheffield, Southampton,
St Andrews, Warwick, York
Please check with your university
careers service for details of events.

Application deadline
Year-round recruitment

Contact Details
✉ contacthr@cliffordchance.com
☎ 020 7006 6006
Turn to page 200 now to request more
information about Clifford Chance.

Clifford Chance is a truly global law firm, which operates as one organisation throughout the world. Their aim is to provide the highest quality professional advice by combining technical expertise with an appreciation of the commercial environment in which their clients work.

As trainee lawyers, graduates will gain breadth and depth in their experiences. Clifford Chance offers a uniquely global perspective and actively encourage their lawyers to develop international experience. Most trainees interested in an international secondment spend six months abroad.

With offices in 20 countries, the firm operates across all business cultures and offers full service advice to clients in key financial and regulatory centres in Europe, the Americas and Asia. Clifford Chance's lawyers advise internationally and domestically, under both common and civil law systems. Their working style is characterised by a real sense of energy, enthusiasm, and determination to provide the best possible service to their clients.

Clifford Chance's recruitment strategy is based on a long-term view. They want graduates to stay with them on qualification, and enjoy a rewarding career contributing to the success of the global business. They are a diverse multicultural firm and expect and encourage their trainees to develop in directions that reflect their individual talents and style. Throughout their training contract, the firm will give trainees the opportunity to realise their highest ambitions and become part of their commitment to be the world's premier law firm.

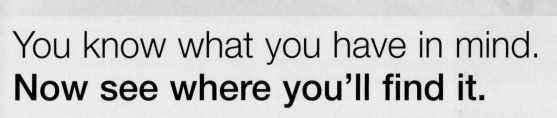

You know what you have in mind.
Now see where you'll find it.

Clifford Chance Limited Liability Partnership

What do you want from your future? A career exploring the kind of opportunities that only one of the world's most successful and respected law firms can offer? To receive outstanding training and rewards? To do interesting and important work that helps shape the face of global commerce? To work with exceptional, down-to-earth people who share a passion for law and are committed to your success? To play an important part in the community and achieve your highest ambitions?

Given the choice, wouldn't you want it all?

To find out more about a career in law at Clifford Chance, visit **www.cliffordchance.com/gradsuk**

THE TIMES
GRADUATE RECRUITMENT
AWARDS 2006
EMPLOYER OF CHOICE

Graduate Employer of Choice
for Law – 2005 and 2006

CLIFFORD
CHANCE

We have a global commitment to diversity, dignity and inclusiveness.

corus

www.corusgroupcareers.com

Vacancies for around 140 graduates in 2007

■ Engineering
■ Finance
■ Human Resources
■ Marketing
■ Purchasing
■ Research & Development
■ Sales

Starting salary for 2007
£19,000-£21,000

Universities that Corus plans to visit in 2006-7

Bath, Birmingham, Bristol, Cambridge, Cardiff, Durham, Lancaster, Leeds, Leicester, Liverpool, London, Loughborough, Manchester, Newcastle, Northumbria, Nottingham, Oxford, Sheffield, Strathclyde, Swansea, Warwick
Please check with your university careers service for details of events.

Application deadline
See website for full details.

Contact Details
✉ recruitment@corusgroup.com
☎ 01926 488025
Turn to page 200 now to request more information about Corus.

Corus will provide the opportunity to learn, develop, gain experience and broaden horizons. Corus have the scope to provide individually tailored careers that will be interesting, challenging and dynamic with commitment to professional accreditation and real work projects from the outset. The starting package includes; competitive salary, bonus, interest free loan and 35 days holiday.

In order to maintain the position as a world class company, people who can set goals and surpass them are essential; with drive, enthusiasm, ideas and flexibility. Successful graduates benchmark their own achievements against those of peers, respect the community around them and simply work hard.

Corus is renowned for creating value. Company culture is one of continuous improvement and open communication with a strong focus on safety and sustainability. Efforts and commitment of Corus employees in 2005 resulted in turnover of £10.3 billion, underlying operating profit of £720 million and a place in the FTSE 100.

Innovative projects Corus are involved in include the elimination of hexavalent chromium in consumer goods which causes white rust, a new "Munchbox" – a safe and hygenic lunchbox for children and steel protective barriers at Westminister for security critical situations. The Sky Plaza in Hong Kong, Ashburton Grove (the new Arsenal stadium), Terminal 3 at Charles de Gaul Airport in Paris and New Bank of America Building in New York all have Corus expertise in common.

Not without You

Corus Expertise and metal helped develop the new Bugatti Veyron, the Sky Plaza in Hong Kong, and NASA Space Shuttles.

We are currently involved in projects such as Ashburton Grove (the new Arsenal stadium), the Fusionpolis landmark in Singapore, Delhi metro in India and new Bank of America Building in New York. To help us maintain our position as a world class company, we recruit into 10 different areas, varying from Engineering to Commercial and Supplies Management to RD&T to Finance – to name but a few. To take the company forward successfully we need people who have drive, enthusiasm, ideas, commitment, imagination and flexibility.

In return we offer a renowned training and development plan tailored to your individual needs with opportunities to learn, develop, gain experience and make your mark.

All applications are on line. To find out more about how Corus can meet your aspirations, and to register your interest in a graduate career or undergraduate placement, please visit our website. The starting package includes competitive salary with bonus, 35 days holiday, employee share save schemes and interest free loan.

For more information about a career with Corus, call our recruitment hotline – 01926 488025

www.corusgroupcareers.com

CREDIT SUISSE

Vacancies for around
160-180 **graduates in 2007**

- Finance
- Investment Banking
- IT

Starting salary for 2007
£Competitive

Universities Credit Suisse plans to visit in 2006-7
Please check with your university careers service for details of events.

Application deadline
24th November 2006

Contact Details
✉ graduate.recruitment@credit-suisse.com
Turn to page 200 now to request more information about Credit Suisse.

Credit Suisse is a leading global financial services organisation headquartered in Zurich. Its business is focused on serving clients in investment banking, private banking and asset management. Credit Suisse is renowned for providing expert advice, holistic solutions and innovative products to a wide range of corporate and institutional clients and high-net-worth individuals globally.

Five areas within the investment banking division recruit graduates: the investment banking department; fixed income; equities; shared services; and information technology.

Credit Suisse considers its training to be truly exceptional in every area. Graduates who join on a full-time basis can expect a one to two month in-depth development program upfront, followed by ongoing on-the-job and division-specific training. The more focused and motivated the graduate is, the faster they will develop. In information technology and shared services, training is hands-on, so after an initial three-week induction the graduates get straight into their role, with structured follow-on technical and professional skills training.

Credit Suisse people come from a wide range of backgrounds and cultures, with degrees in different subjects and aspirations to take their careers in different directions. But there are certain common qualities. They are people who are open-minded about work, life and their future; who get a buzz out of approaching problems differently; and who know there's always something greater to be achieved. They're people who stand out in all sorts of ways and, as a result, fit into Credit Suisse.

Some think
it's about being
competitive.

**We think
it's about being
collaborative.**

Working for an investment bank is demanding enough
without having to constantly prove you're better than the
next person. Particularly when it's much more rewarding to
learn from each other, pool ideas and build on combined
strengths. If you thrive on teamwork, you'll get on faster
here, whatever your background, nationality, culture or
degree discipline. www.credit-suisse.com/standout

Thinking New Perspectives.

CREDIT SUISSE

Vacancies for around
25 **graduates in 2007**

 IT

Starting salary for 2007
£28,000
Plus £4,000 joining bonus.

Universities that
Data Connection
plans to visit in 2006-7
Cambridge, Durham,
Edinburgh, Loughborough,
Oxford, St Andrews,
Warwick
Please check with your university
careers service for details of events.

Application deadline
Year-round recruitment

Contact Details
 recruit@dataconnection.com
☎ 020 8366 1177

Turn to page 200 now to request more
information about Data Connection.

Data Connection has a culture that rewards talent and
dedication, and values innovation and entrepreneurial spirit.
Their passion is the development of their people, who benefit
from early responsibility and unparalleled investment in training.
The company has been voted in the top 5 of the Sunday Times
'100 Best Companies to Work For' for the third consecutive year.

Data Connection is one of the world's leading technology companies.
Organisations like IBM, Microsoft and Cisco use Data Connection's technology
to help their products drive the world's communication networks.

The company recruits highly ambitious and motivated individuals from any
discipline, with all 'A' grade A levels. They care passionately about employee
development and believe in taking talented individuals, nurturing them, and
working with them to fulfil their potential. World Class Technical Expert.
Product Manager. Marketing Professional. Director of Sales. Chief Executive.
Data Connection will help each individual get there, providing they have the
drive and ability. Their policy of promoting from within means that almost all of
their senior executives joined them as graduates.

Graduates will join them on £32,000 (a starting remuneration of £28,000, plus a
signing-on bonus of £4,000). The company is owned by an Employee Benefit
Trust, which means that all the profit the company makes each year (currently
£9 million) is distributed to every employee in accordance with their
contribution.

They also offer an attractive benefits package including non-contributory
pension and private medical insurance, and a few specials of their own,
including regular company outings (e.g. Rome in 2006).

GRADUATE OPPORTUNITIES | £28K + £4K JOINING BONUS

HOW DO YOU BECOME ONE OF THE TOP FIVE PLACES TO WORK IN THE UK THREE YEARS RUNNING (SUNDAY TIMES TOP 100)? HOW DO YOU ATTRACT THE SHARPEST, MOST CREATIVE AND INQUISITIVE MINDS TO SOLVE SOME OF THE MOST COMPLEX PROBLEMS FACING NEXT GENERATION TECHNOLOGY? BY INVESTING. CONTINUALLY. AT DATA CONNECTION, WE NEVER STOP THINKING OF WAYS TO PUT MORE INTO NOT JUST OUR TECHNOLOGY, BUT ALSO OUR PEOPLE. WE SUPPORT, WE TRAIN, WE REWARD. WE OFFER AN INDUSTRY RENOWNED BENEFITS PACKAGE AND WE DO ALL OF IT WITH TWO THINGS IN MIND: YOU AND YOUR DEVELOPMENT. IF YOU'RE THE KIND OF PERSON WHO NEVER STOPS ASKING, START DOING IT WITH DATA CONNECTION. VISIT WWW.DATACONNECTION.COM TO FIND HOW. AND WHY. AND WHERE. AND WHAT...

Deloitte.

www.deloitte.co.uk/graduates

Vacancies for around
1,200 graduates in 2007

- Accountancy
- Consulting
- Finance
- IT

Starting salary for 2007
£Competitive

Universities that Deloitte
plans to visit in 2006-7
Aberdeen, Aston, Bath,
Belfast, Birmingham, Bristol,
Cambridge, Cardiff, City,
Dublin, Durham, East
Anglia, Edinburgh, Exeter,
Glasgow, Heriot-Watt,
Lancaster, Leeds, Leicester,
Liverpool, London,
Loughborough, Manchester,
Newcastle, Nottingham,
Oxford, Reading, Sheffield,
Southampton, St Andrews,
Strathclyde, Warwick, York
Please check with your university
careers service for details of events.

Application deadline
Year-round recruitment

Contact Details
✉ gradrec.uk@deloitte.co.uk
☎ 0800 323 333

Turn to page 200 now to request
more information about Deloitte.

Deloitte offers graduates a challenging, but highly rewarding career within the professional services industry. The depth and breadth of their expertise allows them to offer their clients an unrivalled service. They're a world-class firm with a network of UK offices and an abundance of career paths and opportunities.

Talent is the lifeblood of the firm. Deloitte employs people who are great and make them exceptional. The training and development programmes they provide are second-to-none and will guarantee that graduates become highly skilled and well-rounded business professionals. They nurture talent both formally and informally with programmes that are tailor-made for each individual. From the Summer Vacation Scheme to their workshadow days, there are many ways to find out what working with Deloitte is really like, even before graduation.

Deloitte has a huge number of bright individuals working for them in the UK. All that talent and flair makes Deloitte a particularly invigorating place to be. Their culture encourages that rare state of equilibrium where hard work really is balanced by enjoying a life outside of work. They believe in plain speaking, pragmatic thinking and delivering on their promises, both to one another and to their clients. All of which makes Deloitte a special place to work.

Deloitte recruits graduates with a minimum of 300 UCAS tariff points and a predicted or obtained 2:1 in any discipline. Deloitte welcomes applications for deferred entry.

Apply online at www.deloitte.co.uk/graduates. For Consulting only, the deadline is 31st January 2007.

Peter once imagined he could be Mr Universe.

Now he's proved his strength on the sale of Fitness First.

Ambition is a good thing. So are aspirations. Ours have helped to keep us ahead in the global marketplace for professional services. It's the ambition of exceptional individuals like you that has helped us achieve our goals. Like the expert valuation and unprecedented market insights we provided for this leisure group. For you, it's the promise of a career that can take you further - and faster - than you ever thought possible.

www.deloitte.co.uk/graduates

A career worth aspiring to

Deloitte.

Audit . Tax . Consulting . Corporate Finance .

Deutsche Bank

www.db.com/careers

Vacancies for around
1,000 graduates in 2007

 Finance

 Human Resources

Investment Banking

 IT

Starting salary for 2007
£30,000+

Universities Deutsche Bank
plans to visit in 2006-7
Please check with your university
careers service for details of events.

Application deadline
1st November 2006

Contact Details
☎ 020 7545 3033

Turn to page 200 now to request more
information about Deutsche Bank.

Deutsche Bank has been a global player for more than 135 years, from financing the building of the Baghdad Railway in the 19th century to being the first German bank to list on the NYSE in 2001. Today, it is a financial services provider, top executor of M&A deals, Europe's number 1 fund manager and the global leader in securities trading.

At Deutsche Bank 'A Passion to Perform' is more than just a claim, it is the way it does business, attracting the brightest talent to deliver an unmatched franchise. Deutsche Bank's breadth of experience, leading-edge capabilities and financial strength create value for all its stakeholders: clients, investors, employees, and society as a whole.

The Deutsche Bank training programmes are designed not only to develop business and technical skills but also to facilitate integration into a global culture.

The training programme starts with the Global Orientation in London. This is followed by a teambuilding event, designed to develop graduates' ability to work across national, cultural and divisional boundaries. The classroom based training is a structured cycle of experience and review, during which participants will achieve measurable development in knowledge and skills.

Deutsche Bank is looking for fresh innovative minds, creative spirits and a hunger to succeed. Successful applicants will strive to take ownership of their own projects and they will reap the rewards the bank offers them as a result of their success.

**Your vision: To reach for the top.
Our promise: Lifting you even higher.**

You thrive on achievement and you want to see just how far your talent will take you. We do too. That's why, at Deutsche Bank, you'll be given the opportunity to realize your greatest ambitions. As one of the world's leading financial institutions, we have the platform to take your career higher. You will be part of an innovative, modern corporate culture that celebrates achievement. We have graduate and internship opportunities across a wide range of careers – find out more at www.db.com/careers

Expect the better career.

A Passion to Perform.   **Deutsche Bank**

DLA PIPER

www.dlapiper.com

Vacancies for around 90 graduates in 2007
For training contracts starting in 2009

■ Law

Starting salary in 2006
£18,000-£31,000

Universities that DLA Piper plans to visit in 2006-7
Aberdeen, Birmingham, Bristol, Cambridge, Cardiff, Dundee, Durham, Edinburgh, Exeter, Glasgow, Hull, Leeds, Leicester, Liverpool, London, Manchester, Newcastle, Nottingham, Oxford, Sheffield, St Andrews, Strathclyde, Warwick, York
Please check with your university careers service for details of events.

Application deadline
31st July 2007

Contact Details
✉ recruitment.graduate
   @dlapiper.com
☎ 020 7796 6677

Turn to page 200 now to request more information about DLA Piper.

DLA Piper is one of the world's largest business law firms. Over 3,000 lawyers across 59 offices in 22 countries provide a broad range of legal services through their global practice groups. The firm is built to meet the ongoing needs of clients, wherever they choose to do business. These clients include some of the world's leading businesses, governments, banks and financial institutions.

The firm holds the 'Investors in People' accreditation, demonstrating commitment to its employees and their ongoing development. DLA Piper has an extensive Corporate Social Responsibility programme to support local communities around each office, this includes pro-bono work as well as educational and environmental projects and trainees are encouraged to get involved as a way of developing themselves personally and professionally.

DLA Piper welcomes applications from candidates with either a law or non-law background who have a minimum of 3 Bs at A Level and a 2.1 degree classification (expected or achieved). The firm looks for highly motivated and energetic team players with sound commercial awareness, outstanding communication and organisational skills, and, above all, an appetite for life!

Trainees complete four six-month seats and progress is monitored through regular reviews and feedback. The in-house Professional Skills Course, tailored to the needs of DLA Piper's trainees, combined with high-quality on-the-job experience means each trainee gains an excellent grounding on which to build their professional career.

A formal summer vacation scheme runs throughout the UK offices each year, 200 places are available.

Be different...   Be yourself...

Be part of...

DLA Piper – one of the largest global legal services organisations in the world – and we're still growing! Our impressive client base, combined with the emphasis on high quality service and teamwork, provide a challenging fast paced working environment.

We have offices in Birmingham, Edinburgh, Glasgow, Leeds, Liverpool, London, Manchester and Sheffield as well as 51 international locations in a further 21 countries across Asia, Europe and the US. Our current vision is to be the leading global business law firm.

To find out more about our summer vacation placement scheme or our training contracts, please visit our website **www.dlapiper.com**

DLA Piper adheres to the Law Society's Voluntary Code to Good Practice in the Recruitment of Trainee Solicitors

INVESTOR IN PEOPLE

DLA PIPER

[dstl]

www.dstl.gov.uk/careers

Vacancies for around 100 graduates in 2007

■ Engineering
■ Research & Development

Starting salary for 2007
£Competitive

Universities that Dstl plans to visit in 2006-7

Bath, Birmingham, Bristol, Cambridge, Durham, Edinburgh, Exeter, Lancaster, Leeds, London, Loughborough, Manchester, Nottingham, Oxford, Sheffield, Southampton, St Andrews, Surrey, Strathclyde, Warwick, York
Please check with your university careers service for details of events.

Application deadline
See website for full details.

Contact Details
✉ graduates@dstl.gov.uk
☎ 01980 614596
Turn to page 200 now to request more information about Dstl.

Make the most of the letters after your name.

Dstl, the Defence Science and Technology Laboratory, delivers breakthrough scientific and technological solutions to the Ministry of Defence and wider government.

At Dstl, 3,500 of the finest scientists and technologists in their fields working in world-class research facilities are delivering projects that matter to millions. Through groundbreaking defence research, specialist technical services and the tracking of global technological developments, they support UK Armed Forces, combat threats to our national security and prepare us for tomorrow's military challenges. However, Dstl has taken its expertise beyond defence to deliver ingenious solutions in areas such as health.

Intellectually curious, analytically minded graduates are given huge scope to put academic theory into practice and push back the boundaries of knowledge. They are recruited from a range of disciplines: applied sciences, physical sciences, engineering, biological & health sciences, systems analysis and operational research. All will be flexible self-starters who can work independently or within a team.

Dstl offers a Chartership scheme to help graduates gain membership of a relevant professional body, full support for further qualifications and a 'buddy' scheme. Through partnerships with industry and NATO allies, UK and overseas secondments are also a realistic prospect. Dstl also provides fully flexible working patterns, childcare support and on-site sporting and social activities to ensure a fulfilling work/life balance. Salaries are designed to attract high achievers and, as civil servants, graduates receive comprehensive benefits including a choice of pension schemes.

Use your BSc

to become a VIP

in defence S&T.

INVESTOR IN PEOPLE

[dstl]

Dstl is part of the Ministry of Defence

Make the most of the letters after your name.

ЕⅡ ERNST & YOUNG

www.ey.com/uk/graduate

Vacancies for around 650 graduates in 2007

- Accountancy
- Consulting
- Finance
- Investment Banking
- IT

Starting salary for 2007
£Competitive

Universities Ernst & Young plans to visit in 2006-7

Aberdeen, Aston, Bath, Birmingham, Bristol, Brunel, Cambridge, Cardiff, City, Durham, Edinburgh, Exeter, Glasgow, Heriot-Watt, Lancaster, Leeds, Liverpool, London, Loughborough, Manchester, Newcastle, Nottingham, Oxford, Reading, Sheffield, Southampton, St Andrews, Strathclyde, Ulster, Warwick, York
Please check with your university careers service for details of events.

Application deadline
Year-round recruitment

Contact Details
✉ gradrec@uk.ey.com
☎ 0800 289 208

Turn to page 200 now to request more information about Ernst & Young.

Ernst & Young is one of the leading professional services firms globally with offices in 140 countries worldwide and with more than 100,000 employees. It is a fascinating environment and an excellent place to learn how businesses really work as they help business leaders to tackle their most challenging issues.

The graduate programme offers career opportunities in the following areas: audit, tax, corporate finance and advisory services. Each course of comprehensive training varies depending on which graduate programme is chosen – pursue a professional qualification or work more broadly across the advisory businesses gaining varied experiences. All graduates work closely with a senior level mentor acting as a guide within the firm from day one. Graduates will be working with a team of experienced people in client teams, learning on the job and identifying the specialised training that aims to help them reach career goals sooner.

As a graduate it's not just a matter of knowledge. It's about a working attitude. Ernst & Young are looking for graduates who share their ambition to succeed and bring quality to everything they do. Successful applicants will be provided with unprecedented opportunities to drive and shape the direction of their career.

Ernst & Young appreciates that it is difficult to make a decision about the future without all the facts. That's why they offer undergraduates the opportunity to work with and get to know the firm, and experience the job before committing. This experience can be gained from the first year at university, through the firm's Easter Work Experience Programme, or through the more concentrated experience of Summer Internships and Industrial Placement Programmes.

Ernst & Young wants its graduates to realise their full potential and help make a real difference to businesses.

Getinsidebusiness

Build better business from the inside.
Explore a career with Ernst & Young.

www.ey.com/uk/graduate

EVERSHEDS

**Vacancies for around
80 graduates in 2007**
For training contracts starting in 2009

 Law

Starting salary for 2007
£29,000

**Universities Eversheds
plans to visit in 2006-7**
Aberystwyth, Belfast,
Birmingham, Bristol,
Cambridge, Cardiff, Dublin,
Dundee, Durham, East
Anglia, Edinburgh, Essex,
Exeter, Glasgow, Hull,
Keele, Lancaster, Leeds,
Leicester, Liverpool,
London, Manchester,
Newcastle, Northumbria,
Nottingham, Oxford,
Reading, Sheffield,
St Andrews, Warwick, York
Please check with your university
careers service for details of events.

Application deadline
31st July 2007

Contact Details
✉ gradrec@eversheds.com

Turn to page 200 now to request
more information about Eversheds.

Eversheds LLP is one of the largest full service international law firms in the world with over 4,000 people and over 2,100 legal advisers. With 28 offices in major cities across the UK, Europe and Asia, Eversheds provides services to private and public sector businesses and the finance community.

Eversheds are ranked 3rd in relation to the number of FTSE 250 clients that they act for (source: Chambers Client report, November 2005). Eversheds has always challenged the trends of traditional law firms and prides itself on being client centred as well as a great place to work.

At Eversheds trainees are treated differently. From day one they are given the chance to make a real difference, giving them a positive experience and the chance to continually develop. The firm's trainees are given as much responsibility as they can handle and benefit from the hands on, learning-by-doing philosophy that Eversheds holds. The trainees' learning and development is taken very seriously but it is fun too!

Trainees are appointed both a supervisor and a mentor to assist them throughout their training contract. During the four six month seats, which will cover the firm's main practice areas, they will participate from an early stage in varied, complex and high-value work. There are also many opportunities to be seconded either to another Eversheds office or to a client. During the training contract trainees will also complete an Eversheds designed professional skills course.

A law firm where you'll really get stuck in

Real work, real challenge, real progress

At Eversheds we'll be giving you responsibility straight away. Our trainees work for international names on jobs that make the headlines. We'll provide you with a career that challenges and stimulates you.

You will be supported by a training and development programme that helps you match your talents to your career path. You'll enjoy working for an employer who understands you as an individual and invests in your future.

If you're interested in joining one of the world's largest law firms where you can make a real difference, then find out more by visiting our website at **www.eversheds.com**

 EVERSHEDS

www.eversheds.com

ExxonMobil

Vacancies for around
100 graduates in 2007

- Engineering
- Finance
- Human Resources
- IT
- Marketing
- Sales

Starting salary for 2007
£Competitive

Universities ExxonMobil plans to visit in 2006-7
Aberdeen, Bath, Cambridge, Edinburgh, Heriot-Watt, Imperial London, Manchester, Nottingham, Strathclyde, Surrey
Please check with your university careers service for details of events.

Application deadline
Year-round recruitment

Contact Details
Turn to page 200 now to request more information about ExxonMobil.

ExxonMobil is the world's largest publicly traded international oil and gas company with a presence in nearly 200 countries and territories. They are an industry leader in every aspect of the energy and petrochemicals business.

Exxon Mobil Corporation is the parent company of the Esso, Mobil and ExxonMobil companies that operate in the United Kingdom. The business is a truly diverse organisation that offers equally diverse career opportunities. Their customers are both global and local, ranging from major airlines to the individuals who visit our service stations worldwide.

A broad range of career opportunities are available within both commercial and technical functions where graduates can expect immediate responsibility and accountability. Analytical skills are essential, as is the ability to think, act and adapt in a global environment with sound judgment and tenacity.

The two-year ExxonMobil Graduate Development Programme is run in conjunction with the London Business School (LBS) covering interpersonal skills, business awareness and people management leading to alumni status of the LBS.

Input from supervisors helps graduates develop an appropriate career path by reviewing their skills and training needs. All graduates develop technical and personal skills via internal and external courses, and on-the-job training. Graduates are also encouraged to achieve chartered qualifications where appropriate.

Rapid skills growth and career development is standard and graduates can expect a high degree of intellectual challenge and change.

5 billion people in the developing world still lack access to modern energy supplies.

www.exxonmobil.com/ukrecruitment

Your ideas could be the key to a much brighter future.

It's an economic fact. Society cannot advance without adequate supplies of energy – energy that powers homes, harvests crops, and improves lives. It's a huge challenge. On the one hand, the world demands more and more energy. On the other, it demands less and less environmental impact.

Welcome to the world of ExxonMobil. A place where people are working together right now to address the world's toughest energy challenges.

The need for energy is increasing rapidly – in just 25 years the world will require as much as 50% more energy than today. At ExxonMobil your ideas can make the difference. We're pursuing new sources of energy, we're developing more efficient fuel and engine systems, and we're investing in people just like you.

The biggest challenges attract the best. Whether your background is in business, engineering, or science, ExxonMobil has a challenging career waiting for you.

 **Mobil**

ExxonMobil
Taking on the world's toughest energy challenges.™

Vacancies for around
60 **graduates in 2007**

Finance

Starting salary for 2007
£27,500

Universities that the Financial Services Authority plans to visit in 2006-7
Aston, Bath, Birmingham, Bristol, Cambridge, Durham, Edinburgh, London, Manchester, Nottingham, Oxford, Reading, Sheffield, Warwick
Please check with your university careers service for details of events.

Application deadline
7th January 2007

Contact Details
Turn to page 200 now to request more information about the Financial Services Authority.

www.fsa.gov.uk/careers

The role of the Financial Services Authority (FSA) is to help the UK financial services industry work effectively, delivering benefits to firms and consumers alike. From getting a fair deal for everyone in their financial affairs to maintaining London's status as a world-leading international financial centre, the FSA's remit is broad and their influence profound.

As such, their graduates enjoy an unrivalled overview of one of the UK's most complex and critical industries. Setting and monitoring standards for an industry comprising 29,000 financial companies of all sizes; providing key services and information to firms and consumers alike; explaining judgments and decisions to everyone from the media to Parliament: FSA graduates experience it all.

What's more, genuine responsibility is given to graduates from day one of the two-and-a-half year graduate development programme. From there, two internal rotations and a six-month external secondment provide a unique breadth of insight into the world of financial services. All the while, an impressive array of training courses and qualifications ensures ongoing professional and personal development.

By the end of it, FSA graduates are ready to step straight into a long and rewarding career at the heart of the industry – and to make a real difference, both in the City of London and throughout the country.

To find out what it takes to be a financial services authority, and to apply online, visit www.fsa.gov.uk/careers

Investment Banks

 Retail Banks

 Insurance and Mortgage Brokers

 Insurance Companies

 Investment Management

Why settle for a single slice?

No one sees more of the financial services world than we do. As the sole UK regulator, we're here to ensure fairness, integrity and efficiency across all aspects of the industry. And that makes our graduate development programme the perfect way to get a bigger slice of the action. Find out how at **www.fsa.gov.uk/careers**

FSA

THE FINANCIAL SERVICES AUTHORITY

FRESHFIELDS BRUCKHAUS DERINGER

www.freshfields.com/graduates

**Vacancies for around
100 graduates in 2007**

For training contracts starting in 2009

Law

Starting salary for 2007
£31,000

**Universities Freshfields
Bruckhaus Deringer
plans to visit in 2006-7**

Birmingham, Bristol,
Cambridge, Cardiff,
Durham, Edinburgh, Exeter,
Glasgow, Leeds, Leicester,
Liverpool, London,
Manchester, Newcastle,
Northumbria, Nottingham,
Oxford, Sheffield,
St Andrews, Warwick

Please check with your university
careers service for details of events.

Application deadline
31st July 2007

Contact Details

✉ graduates@freshfields.com

☎ 020 7427 3194

Turn to page 200 now to request
more information about Freshfields
Bruckhaus Deringer.

Freshfields Bruckhaus Deringer is a leading international law
firm. Through its network of 28 offices in 18 countries, the firm
provides first-rate legal services to corporations, financial
institutions and governments around the world.

The firm's lawyers work on high profile, interesting and often ground-breaking
work for clients such as Kingfisher, BT, LVMH, DaimlerChrysler, Deutsche
Bank, P&O and the Bank of England.

The firm recruits about 100 people each year to start as trainee solicitors
in its London office. The firm has a thriving practice in practically all
commercial areas, and it is recognised as a market leader for a wide
range of work.

There is no such thing as a 'typical' Freshfields lawyer. The firm's broad
array of practice areas and clients demands a wide range of individuals with
differing skills, abilities and interests. Successful candidates will require
strong academic qualifications, a broad range of skills and a good record of
achievement in other areas.

The firm's trainees receive a thorough professional training in an extensive
range of practice areas, an excellent personal development programme and
the chance to work in one of its international offices or on secondment with a
client in the UK or abroad.

The firm has 100 places on its Easter and summer vacation schemes for
penultimate year undergraduates. Applications for places in 2007 should be
made between 20th November 2006 and 19th January 2007.

Shahab, trainee

RELENTLESS.

THE TRAINING, NOT THE WORKLOAD.

We won't deny that joining us is a tough challenge. This is one of the world's biggest and most successful law firms and our clients have expectations to match.

But that doesn't mean we leave our new graduates to sink or swim – quite the opposite. Our training and support is as varied and wide-ranging as our business. And it doesn't just stop at qualifying, but continues virtually non-stop throughout your career.

To find out more about our graduate opportunities go to:

www.freshfields.com/graduates

 FRESHFIELDS BRUCKHAUS DERINGER

FUJITSU

Vacancies for around
100 graduates in 2007

- Accountancy
- Consulting
- General Management
- Human Resources
- IT
- Marketing
- Purchasing
- Sales

Vacancies also available in Europe.

Starting salary for 2007
£24,000

Universities that Fujitsu
plans to visit in 2006-7
Aston, Bath, Birmingham,
Lancaster, Leeds, Liverpool,
Loughborough, Manchester,
Nottingham, Reading,
Sheffield, Swansea, Warwick
Please check with your university
careers service for details of events.

Application deadline
31st January 2007

Contact Details
Turn to page 200 now to request
more information about Fujitsu.

The qualities Fujitsu seeks in its graduates are the same qualities that their customers seek in them. The ability to stand out from the crowd, to offer something different and to go that extra mile to achieve success. It's how they've built a solid reputation.

Fujitsu's no-nonsense, straightforward approach to business and IT means that their customers are many of Europe's leading companies. In addition, Fujitsu Services is the number one IT services provider to the UK government.

Fujitsu are looking for people who will not only enhance their reputation but who have the potential to make a strong contribution to extending and expanding their success. They provide a comprehensive eighteen-month development programme to give all graduate entrants the generic business skills required to operate effectively as leaders of the future.

Fujitsu are keen for successful applicants to play an active part in the organisation as quickly as possible. Everything is done to help graduates settle in smoothly. The company has a buddy system that pairs graduates up with someone in their immediate working area, probably a previous graduate, who will be on hand to help with day-to-day issues. Then graduates will have a mentor, an experienced manager, who they meet several times a year to discuss their progression, to understand their strengths and to help plan their career course. Graduates are invited to attend regular events, which offer the chance to compare notes and socialise.

As the European arm of the world's third largest IT company and with revenues in excess of £2.5 billion, Fujitsu is securing a long-term future for both their business and their people. For the chance to stand out in an outstanding company, apply now!

To be **successful**
you have to be **different**.

You could just **follow** the crowd,
or **stand out** from them.

What do
you want to do?

Vacancies for around
200 **graduates in 2007**

▮ General Management
▮ IT

Starting salary for 2007
£21,196

**Universities that GCHQ
plans to visit in 2006-7**
Please check with your university
careers service for details of events.

Application deadline
Year-round recruitment

Contact Details
✉ recruitment@gchq.gsi.gov.uk

Turn to page 200 now to request
more information about GCHQ.

GCHQ (Government Communications Headquarters) is part of
British Intelligence and works closely with MI5 and MI6 to counter
the numerous threats, which face the nation and global community.

Using some of the world's most sophisticated technology, they intercept
communications and electronic signals which teams help turn into raw intelligence.
Their reports reach the very top of government and can be used to inform foreign
policy decisions, or used in combating terrorism, drugs trafficking, the proliferation
of weapons of mass destruction and international crime.

GCHQ is also charged with preventing hostile forces compromising the
UK's critical communications infrastructure. This is the responsibility of CESG
(the UK National Technical Authority for Information Assurance), a key division
within the business. Together, they employ around 4,500 people; mainly at
the HQ in Cheltenham.

Like any large and complex business, a diverse range of people and skills are
needed. While many of these are typical of most organisations (finance,
administration, audit), GCHQ's wider role is unique. And so are the types of
people they recruit. These include IT and telecommunications specialists to
maintain and develop capabilities; linguists to monitor and translate a variety
of communications; mathematicians to help set and crack codes;
librarians/information specialists to provide back-up research; and
Intelligence Analysts to piece together information.

Everyone benefits from personalised training, support towards professional
qualifications, mentoring, and shadowing. GCHQ's campaigns run throughout the
year, please check the website for more details. Applicants must be British citizens.

GCHQ

SECRET

AS ONE OF THE UK'S THREE INTELLIGENCE SERVICES, WE OPERATE
ON A STRICTLY NEED TO KNOW BASIS.

Which means ████████████████ exciting
████████████████████████ protect Britain
and British ██████████████ terrorism, computer crime and illegal
████████████████████   ████████████

████████████ award-winning HQ in Cheltenham
████████████ computing superpower, ████████ first-class
facilities. Graduates enjoy ████████████████ training and
████████████████ explore careers in ████████████
professional qualifications.

A civil service organisation ████████████ ████████
diverse community ████████████ 2(2) minimum.
████████████ stimulating careers in a ████████████
████████████ environment.

NEED TO KNOW MORE, ████████ WEBSITE,
████████████ APPLY.

WWW.CAREERSINBRITISHINTELLIGENCE.CO.UK ████████████
TEL: 01242 709095/6

END OF MESSAGE.

APPLICANTS MUST BE BRITISH CITIZENS

GlaxoSmithKline

www.gsk.com/careers

Vacancies for around
40 graduates in 2007

- Accountancy
- Engineering
- Finance
- IT
- Logistics
- Marketing
- Purchasing
- Research & Development
- Sales

Starting salary for 2007
£Competitive

Universities that GSK
plans to visit in 2006-7
Please check with your university
careers service for details of events.

Application deadline
See website for full details.

Contact Details
Turn to page 200 now to request
more information about GSK.

GlaxoSmithKline (GSK) is a place where ideas come to life. As one of the world's leading research-based pharmaceutical companies, GSK is dedicated to delivering products and medicines that help millions of people around the world do more, feel better and live longer.

Based in the UK, but with operations in the US and 115 other countries worldwide, GSK make almost 4 billion packs of medicine and healthcare products every year, with sales of £21.6 billion in 2005. And much of this is thanks to an extensive product range that includes everything from prescription medicines to popular consumer healthcare products.

So while some people depend on GSK's pioneering pharmaceutical products to tackle life-threatening illnesses, others choose best-selling nutritional brands such as Lucozade and Ribena for a feel-good boost. GSK even manages to brighten smiles with some of the world's favourite toothpaste brands.

New starters at GSK will soon see that there's no such thing as a typical career path at GSK. With roles at all levels, as well as a number of industrial placements, across all business functions, there are plenty of opportunities to learn and develop.

And with so much geographical and business diversity on offer, GSK is in a great position to give all the support needed. There are no limits on where a career could lead – their various development programmes in the UK have produced some of GSK's most aspiring leaders. Find out more about the opportunities on offer by visiting GSK at www.gsk.com/careers

www.gsk.com/careers

Improving lives is in our nature, we'll do the same for you.

Graduate Opportunities

Sales and Marketing, Finance, R&D, IT, Purchasing, Regulatory Affairs, Global Manufacturing and Supply

People all over the world look to GlaxoSmithKline for a healthier future, and we take pride in helping them do more, feel better and live longer. But it's not just the people that use our products who get to enjoy everything we have to offer. Our wide-ranging graduate opportunities will give your career the best possible start, whatever your skills may be. And as well as plenty of exposure to major business challenges, you'll also enjoy a competitive salary and personalised benefits package.

For a full listing of current opportunities, please visit our website at www.gsk.com/careers
All data processed in accordance with the provisions of the Data Protection Act.
GSK is proud to promote an open culture, encouraging people to be themselves and giving their ideas a chance to flourish.
GSK is proud to be an equal opportunity employer.

Together we can make life better.

Goldman Sachs

Vacancies for around
250 **graduates in 2007**

- Accountancy
- Finance
- Human Resources
- Investment Banking
- IT

Vacancies also available
in Europe, the USA and Asia.

Starting salary for 2007
£Competitive

**Universities that
Goldman Sachs
plans to visit in 2006-7**
Bath, Birmingham, Bristol,
Cambridge, Dublin, Durham,
Edinburgh, Glasgow, Leeds,
London, Manchester,
Nottingham, Oxford,
Southampton, St Andrews,
Strathclyde, Warwick, York
Please check with your university
careers service for details of events.

Application deadline
10th November 2006

Contact Details
☎ 020 7552 1738

Turn to page 200 now to request more
information about Goldman Sachs.

Goldman Sachs is a global investment banking, securities and investment management firm. It provides a wide range of services to a substantial and diversified client base that includes corporations, financial institutions, governments, non-profit organisations and high-net-worth individuals.

Goldman Sachs welcomes graduates from a wide range of university courses and backgrounds. There are a number of different stages when graduates can consider joining Goldman Sachs. Naturally, these will offer different degrees of exposure and responsibility but whether graduates join as interns, new analysts or associates, they will immediately become part of the team with a real and substantial role to play.

Goldman Sachs recruits the best graduates from a wide range of university courses and backgrounds. Academic discipline is less important than the personal qualities an individual brings with them, however a strong appreciation and interest in finance is important. It is intellect, personality and zest for life that the firm values the most.

Goldman Sachs' ability to meet challenges and ensure the firm's success in the future depends on attracting and retaining the highest quality people and the firm takes an unusual effort to identify the best person for every job. They evaluate candidates on six core measures – achievement, leadership, commercial focus, analytical thinking, teamwork and the ability to make an impact. The firm expects commitment, enthusiasm and drive from its employees but in return, offers unparalleled exposure, early responsibility, significant rewards and unlimited career opportunities.

Enrich your life, not just your career.

Surround yourself with a group of people that can help you grow. You'll be exposed to a range of skills and experiences that you'll come to rely on both professionally and personally, including rigorous training programmes and a mentoring system.

Goldman Sachs is a leading global investment banking, securities and investment management firm that provides a wide range of services worldwide to a substantial and diversified client base that includes corporations, financial institutions, governments, non-profit organisations and high-net-worth individuals.

We offer career opportunities for new analysts and associates. To find out more about our career paths and to complete an online application, please visit **www.gs.com/careers**

Google

www.google.com/jobs

Vacancies for around
100-300 **graduates in 2007**

- Consulting
- General Management
- IT
- Marketing
- Media
- Sales

Vacancies also available
in Asia and Europe.

Starting salary for 2007
£20,000-£35,000
Varies by function and location.

**Universities that Google
plans to visit in 2006-7**
Aberdeen, Aston, Bath,
Belfast, Birmingham, Bristol,
Cambridge, Dublin,
Edinburgh, Leeds,
Liverpool, London,
Manchester, Oxford,
St Andrews, Warwick
Please check with your university
careers service for details of events.

Application deadline
Year-round recruitment

Contact Details
Turn to page 200 now to request
more information about Google.

Google's innovative search technologies connect millions of people around the world with information every day. Google's founders developed a new approach to online search that took root in a university dorm room and quickly spread to information seekers around the globe. Google is now widely recognised as the world's largest search engine.

Google has a work environment like no other. Working at Google means making a positive difference in tens of millions of lives every day. Google are looking to hire graduates who love to critique the design of everyday things, who dream of working for an innovative, world-class organisation.

They hire exceptional people, at all degree levels, Bachelor's, Master's and Ph.D. With offices all over the world including California, New York, Ireland, Britain, Switzerland, India and Japan, Googlers all over the world are working on the same cutting edge solutions. The people at Google love to work on innovative products and believe passionately in the company's mission: to organise the world's information and make it universally accessible and useful.

Positions are available within Engineering, IT, Sales, Client Service and Marketing teams. Google offers career opportunities within a fun, progressive and multicultural environment. Experience is not absolutely essential, but lots of personality is!

Applicants must have a passion for the internet and want to help shape the future of one of the world's most exciting companies.

All current roles are visible on www.google.com/jobs – select the country of choice.

The world's favourite search engine is **searching for you**

Are you ready for the biggest adventure of your life?

Google has established a strong presence in Europe and is expanding its international teams across a range of business areas.

If you have a passion for the internet and want to help shape the future of one of the world's most exciting companies go to www.google.com/jobs and select your country and area of interest to find out more or to apply for one of these great positions.

Grant Thornton

www.grant-thornton.co.uk/careers

Vacancies for around
200 **graduates in 2007**

Accountancy

Starting salary for 2007
£Competitive

**Universities that
Grant Thornton
plans to visit in 2006-7**
Please check with your university
careers service for details of events.

Application deadline
Year-round recruitment

Contact Details
Turn to page 200 now to request more
information about Grant Thornton.

Grant Thornton UK LLP is a leading financial and business adviser with 32 offices nationwide. They are the UK member of Grant Thornton International, one of the world's leading international organisations of independently owned and managed accounting and consulting firms. These firms provide a comprehensive range of business advisory services from around 520 offices in over 110 countries worldwide.

Within the firm graduates can pursue opportunities and qualifications in a wide range of specialisms including: audit and assurance services; business tax and private client services; transfer pricing; corporate finance; forensic and investigation; recovery and reorganisation; risk management services and financial markets.

Grant Thornton's commitment to training is second to none. The initial training, at their dedicated training centre, Bradenham Manor (above), will get successful applicants off to a flying start with general business development as well as the technical skills training required to pass the exams.

Grant Thornton look for graduates who are energetic, enthusiastic and who can apply high degrees of practical intelligence to business challenges. Successful graduates will have a good academic record and be expecting a 2:1 Honours degree, or better, in any discipline. For ACA, CA, CTA and Actuarial training a minimum of 300 UCAS/24 A-level points is required and for ACCA training graduates will need a minimum of 240 UCAS/20 A-level points. All applicants must have a minimum of B grades in GCSE Mathematics and English Language.

COG
COG
COG
COG

Individual

Of course we're not suggesting you'll become a small cog in the wheel at the Big 4.
It's just that at Grant Thornton we like to encourage individual thinking. That's what has helped
us become part of one of the fastest growing international accounting organisations[1].
Right now we're recruiting graduates, so if you're considering your career
visit www.grant-thornton.co.uk/careers

Grant Thornton

Think beyond convention...think beyond the Big 4

OVER 100 COUNTRIES* · CORPORATE FINANCE · FINANCIAL MARKETS CONSULTING
FORENSIC ACCOUNTING · PROJECT FINANCE · RECOVERY & REORGANISATION · AUDIT
RISK MANAGEMENT · TAX · WEALTH CONSULTING

[1]Refers to Grant Thornton International Accounting Bulletin, 2005
*Services are delivered nationally by the member firms of Grant Thornton International, a network of independent firms

HBOSplc

www.hbos-choices.co.uk

Vacancies for around
120-180 **graduates in 2007**

Finance

General Management

Human Resources

Investment Banking

IT

Marketing

Retailing

Sales

Starting salary for 2007
£Competitive

Universities that HBOS plans to visit in 2006-7
Aston, Bath, Bristol, Cardiff, Durham, Edinburgh, Lancaster, Leeds, London, Manchester, Nottingham, Southampton, St Andrews, Warwick, York
Please check with your university careers service for details of events.

Application deadline
Year-round recruitment

Contact Details
✉ hbosgrads@hodes.co.uk
☎ 0870 241 2726

Turn to page 200 now to request more information about HBOS.

HBOS plc was established in September 2001 as a result of a merger between the Bank of Scotland and Halifax plc, forming one of the largest financial services organisations in Europe with 22 million customers.

HBOS is also Europe's fastest growing financial services company – it made a pre tax profit of £4.8 billion in 2005. With assets of over £540 billion it is the UK's largest mortgage and savings provider and a major player in the provision of new current accounts and credit cards. With around 2.3 million private shareholders, HBOS also has the largest private shareholder register in the UK.

There are many graduate schemes available at HBOS, including corporate banking, investment management, asset management, financial markets, actuarial, sales management, HR, IT & technology, marketing, surveyors, risk, finance/audit as well as a wide range of general business roles. All schemes are designed to equip graduates with the skills and qualifications necessary for them to significantly contribute to the business throughout their career.

All schemes are UK-based for two years, with the main locations being Edinburgh, Leeds, Halifax, Bristol and London, although some schemes are based elsewhere in the UK. There is more information about the schemes on their website: www.hbos-choices.co.uk.

HBOS is committed to strengthening the relationships it has with its customers, the 60,000 people it employs and the communities they live in. Every effort is made to contribute to the community, with company initiatives ranging from involvement in local charities to support of national projects such as reducing our impact on the environment.

~~Our yearly profits are £4.1bn.~~

Our yearly profits are £4.8bn.

Graduate Schemes

Because we're growing at such a rapid rate, the people who create our recruitment adverts sometimes find it a bit difficult to keep up with us. And even though that's a real headache for them, we've got no intention of slowing down.

That's something you'll discover when you join one of our graduate schemes. As part of an ever-expanding company with an exciting future ahead of it, you'll be able to grow and develop at exactly the same rate as us. And that's pretty fast.

What's more, we have all sorts of different opportunities available. So whatever it is you're about to finish studying, there's a good chance we've got an area of expertise that will suit both you and your ambitions.

If you're already imagining what it'd be like to share in the success of one of the fastest growing financial organisations in the UK (not to mention get on the nerves of our marketing people), then visit **www.hbos-choices.co.uk** to find out more.

Getting bigger by the day

Equal opportunities for all - our policy is as simple as that.

HSBC ◆X◆

The world's local bank

**Vacancies for around
400 graduates in 2007**

- Finance
- General Management
- Investment Banking
- IT
- Logistics
- Retailing
- Sales

Vacancies also available in Europe,
Asia and elsewhere in the world.

Starting salary for 2007
£Competitive

**Universities that HSBC
plans to visit in 2006-7**
Aberystwyth, Aston, Bangor,
Bath, Belfast, Birmingham,
Bristol, Brunel, Cambridge,
Cardiff, City, Durham,
Edinburgh, Exeter, Glasgow,
Hull, Kent, Lancaster, Leeds,
Leicester, Liverpool,
London, Loughborough,
Manchester, Newcastle,
Northumbria, Nottingham,
Oxford, Sheffield,
Southampton, Warwick,
York
Please check with your university
careers service for details of events.

Application deadline
Varies
See website for full details.

Contact Details
✉ graduateteam@hsbc.com
Turn to page 200 now to request
more information about HSBC.

HSBC is one of the largest banking and financial services organisations in the world. It has a network of around 9,500 offices in 76 countries and territories.

HSBC provides a comprehensive range of financial services to more than 125 million customers: personal financial services; consumer finance; commercial banking; corporate, investment banking and markets; and private banking.

Exceptional graduates of any discipline are recruited onto HSBC's world class training programmes, preparing them for management and executive positions across the business.

These include Actuarial, Business Management Operations, Commercial Management, Executive Management, Insurance Broking, Information Technology, Retail Management, International Management, Investment Banking and Wealth Management, Private Banking and Amanah Finance, HSBC's Islamic banking division. HSBC also offers a range of internships to promising undergraduates.

HSBC is committed to certain key business principles and values. In addition to providing appropriate financial products and following fair, responsible lending policies, HSBC has a strong corporate social responsibility programme that contributes to the everyday life of local communities. Employees are encouraged to get involved in HSBC's many educational and environmental projects across the globe.

To find out more about the opportunities that HSBC can offer, select the programme that is right for you, and apply online, visit:
www.hsbc.com/studentcareers

If everyone thought the same, nothing would ever change.

Everywhere you go, you get a different opinion and a different point of view.

When you talk to more than 125 million customers all over the world, you'd be amazed at what you learn.

At HSBC we employ over a quarter of a million people speaking dozens of different languages. We offer you a world of opportunities to realise your potential, experience first class training, expand your abilities, and reap the rewards of early responsibility.

To find out more about the range of programmes available, visit

www.hsbc.com/studentcareers

The world's local bank

www.ibm.com/employment/uk/graduates

I AM
IBM.

Reasons to work at IBM

IBM is the world's leading information technology and consulting services company, with over 90 years of leadership in helping businesses transform. Their extensive list of clients include British Airways, eBay, HMV, Boots and The Wimbledon Championships. IBM is aligned around a single, focused business model: innovation. They help their clients in many industries apply fresh ideas and new technology in order to deliver business value.

Winner of the 2005 and 2006 'The Times IT Graduate Employer of Choice', IBM can offer graduates a career that stands out in both its scope and in its ability to constantly challenge. IBM has opportunities in many areas of consultancy including IT, business, business modelling, supply chain and logistics, along with opportunities in IT services, software development, finance and sales.

Graduates begin their IBM career with a new hire induction program lasting anything from 3 to 9 weeks. After completion of this, personal, business or technical skills training is provided on an ongoing basis. IBM is committed to creating an inclusive workplace that embraces diversity. They promote a flexible working environment that sets them apart from their competitors. Employees are given the tools to do their job and rewarded on the value they provide – not the time spent in the office.

To be considered, graduates should have achieved or be expecting a 2:1 or higher. IBM looks for people that are adaptable, driven, good team players and have a passion for the area of work they are applying to. In return, they offer a competitive salary, an excellent flexible benefits package and an environment where talented individuals thrive.

WE ARE
IBM

Reason #71 to work at IBM

ibm.com/employment/uk/graduates

Choosing a career is not easy. Choosing which company to work for is even harder. With opportunities in many areas of consultancy including IT, business, business modelling, supply chain and logistics, along with opportunities in IT services, software development and sales, IBM can offer you a career that stands out in both its scope and ability to constantly challenge you.

We offer a competitive salary, an excellent flexible benefits package, a comprehensive induction and training programme and an environment where talented individuals thrive.

Reasons to | join IBM

For more information and to apply, please visit **ibm.com**/employment/uk/graduates

John Lewis

www.jlpjobs.com/graduates

Vacancies for around 15-20 graduates in 2007

■ Retailing

Starting salary for 2007
£21,000

Universities John Lewis plans to visit in 2006-7
Please check with your university careers service for details of events.

Application deadline
Late November 2006

Contact Details

✉ careers@johnlewis.co.uk

Turn to page 200 now to request more information about John Lewis.

John Lewis department stores are part of the John Lewis Partnership, one of the UK's best known retailers and a leading example of a co-owned business. All permanent employees share in the responsibilities and benefits arising from being a co-owner of a successful enterprise.

With 26 existing shops, and a successful multi-channel offer, a major expansion in the number of John Lewis stores is planned over the next few years. As John Lewis is growing, so are the opportunities for a great career.

To be successful, graduates in John Lewis need to have a passion for retailing and for working with people. Strong leadership and team working skills, commercial awareness and real initiative and drive are needed to make the most of this opportunity to have a fast-track retail management career.

Graduates in John Lewis are based in the department stores, initially working with customers and alongside other colleagues. Within weeks, graduates take on responsibility for leading and managing teams within a store. This practical experience is supported with development courses, seminars and individual coaching and mentoring.

Within 12-18 months graduates should be ready to manage their own department within a John Lewis store, taking on accountability for the sales and profits of the department and for the happiness and performance of its team. Graduates in John Lewis can go on to progress their careers into a wide variety of areas, and ultimately to the highest levels of management.

Ambitious?

Drive a multi-million pound sales turnover

Lead a team of more than 30 people

Achieve this within 12-18 months

For more information about graduate opportunities with the **UK's favourite retailer*** visit

jlpjobs.com/graduates

*Verdict survey 2006

John Lewis

JPMorgan 🔷

Vacancies for around
400 graduates in 2007

■ Finance
■ Investment Banking
■ IT

jpmorgan.com/careers

THIS IS WHERE YOU NEED TO BE.

Starting salary for 2007
£Competitive

Universities JPMorgan plans to visit in 2006-7
Bath, Bristol, Cambridge, Dublin, Edinburgh, London, Manchester, Nottingham, Oxford, Warwick
Please check with your university careers service for details of events.

Application deadline
19th November 2006
See website for full details.

Contact Details
Turn to page 200 now to request more information about JPMorgan.

Graduates will find early responsibility and the chance to make a quick impact at JPMorgan. New technologies, fresh ideas, changing markets and a pipeline of high-quality work all unite to make JPMorgan an exhilarating place to work. There has never been a better time to launch a career with JPMorgan.

JPMorgan is the investment banking business of JPMorgan Chase, a leading global financial services firm with assets of more than $1.3 trillion and operations in more than 50 countries. The firm serves the interests of clients who have complex financial needs, whether they are major corporations, governments, private firms, financial institutions, non-profit organisations or even private individuals.

The training programmes combine on-the-job learning with classroom instruction that is on par with the world's finest business schools. Graduates will gain exposure to different parts of the business, giving them a multi-dimensional perspective of the company and helping them decide where they might settle. As a result, successful applicants emerge not only with a thorough grounding in their own business area, but also a broad experience of the wider commercial picture and a range of transferable business skills, from project management to team leadership.

JPMorgan is looking for team players and future leaders with exceptional drive, creativity and interpersonal skills. Impeccable academic credentials are important, but so are achievements outside the classroom. More information and helpful advice about graduate careers and internship opportunities can be found at jpmorgan.com/careers

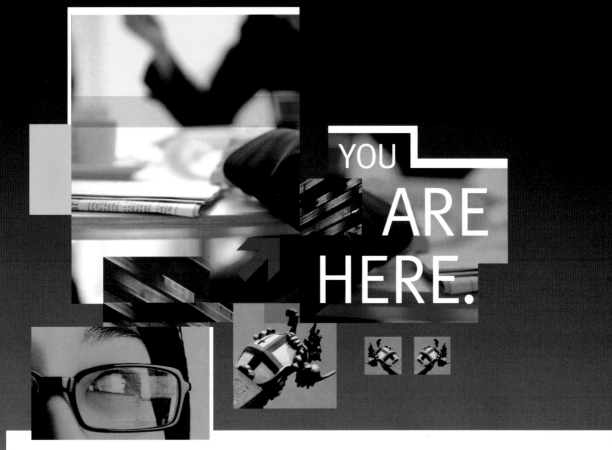

JPMorgan

YOU ARE HERE.

We've spent about two hundred years getting ready for you. We've built an investment bank that does more of the BIG, COMPLEX DEALS than anyone else. We've SET THE PACE OF CHANGE in everything from technology development and product innovation to respect for women at work.

We've created a business platform that meets the global needs of our clients better than anyone else's. And we have created A TEAM SPIRIT that is strong and supportive, without being suffocating or sad. Now we're entering THE MOST EXCITING STAGE OF OUR HISTORY, with investment, GROWTH AND TALENT at the top of the agenda. Even if you've never considered investment banking as a career before, you should now. Because, WHATEVER YOU WANT FROM THE FUTURE — intellectual challenge, personal recognition, professional fulfilment, fast-track development, a richer life, or all of the above - this is where you need to be. THIS IS YOUR TIME.

jpmorgan.com/careers

THIS IS WHERE YOU NEED TO BE.

Vacancies for around 850 graduates in 2007

Accountancy

Finance

Human Resources

IT

Marketing

Sales

Make the best choice for you

Starting salary for 2007
£Competitive

Universities that KPMG plans to visit in 2006-7

Bath, Birmingham, Bristol, Cambridge, Durham, Edinburgh, Glasgow, Leeds, London, Manchester, Newcastle, Nottingham, Oxford, Reading, Sheffield, Strathclyde, Warwick, York
Please check with your university careers service for details of events.

Application deadline
Year-round recruitment

Contact Details

✉ ukfmgraduate@kpmg.co.uk

☎ 0500 664665

Turn to page 200 now to request more information about KPMG.

KPMG is part of an international network of business advisers with almost 100,000 people across their global network in nearly 150 countries. In the UK, they have over 9,000 people and provide clients with audit, tax and advisory services from more than 20 offices.

KPMG is also one of the major employers of graduates in the UK, and offers a wide range of high-quality, challenging careers to people from every academic discipline. There are over 20 different graduate career routes to choose from within KPMG, each of which offers a great balance of structured support and real business challenge. Many of their graduate careers also lead to highly respected and valuable professional qualifications.

In 2005, KPMG was the fastest-growing of the 'Big Four' firms – and they shared the rewards of this success with a market-leading £59 million bonus pool. Just as importantly, they also maintained their track record of consistently exceeding national institutes' average pass rates in professional exams – a testament to both the high-calibre people they recruit and the extensive support they provide at every stage.

KPMG has recently won a number of important awards that recognise both the quality careers they offer their people, and the high level of service they give to clients. These include the CBI's 'Auditor of the Year' and achieving first place in the 2006 Sunday Times 'Best Big Companies To Work For'.

Make the best choice for you

As a student, I did worry that succeeding in a business career meant fundamentally changing who I was, but that hasn't been the case at KPMG. Even in the interview they were interested in my personal achievements just as much as my academic record – and directing a play was actually one of the things that helped me land a job in professional services. Now I'm at KPMG and working directly with clients and tackling real challenges, I can see that a lot of the skills I developed as a director have helped me make an impact in the business environment. Plus, the exams and the work might be tough here – but if you can convince my friend Nick to dress up as a bear, you can probably do anything.

You'll be amazed what you can achieve at KPMG. To find out more about our outstanding business careers, visit **www.kpmg.co.uk/careers** – or, even better, come and meet us face-to-face at one of our campus events.

We are an equal opportunity employer and value diversity in our people.

 KPMG LLP (UK) has been named the country's 'best big company to work for' in the Sunday Times 'best companies' survey. KPMG topped the category for organisations with more than 5,000 employees.

AUDIT ▪ TAX ▪ ADVISORY

L'ORÉAL
WORLD LEADER IN BEAUTY PRODUCTS

www.loréal.co.uk

Vacancies for around 30 graduates in 2007

- Engineering
- Logistics
- Marketing
- Sales

Starting salary for 2007
£Competitive

Universities that L'Oréal plans to visit in 2006-7
Aston, Bath, Bristol, Cambridge, Cardiff, Dublin, Durham, Edinburgh, London, Manchester, Nottingham, Oxford, Swansea, Warwick
Please check with your university careers service for details of events.

Application deadline
Year-round recruitment

Contact Details
Turn to page 200 now to request more information about L'Oréal.

L'Oréal is worldwide number one in cosmetics, launching over 500 new products throughout the world every year. L'Oréal's brand portfolio includes L'Oréal Paris, Lancôme, Maybelline, and Ralph Lauren fragrances.

L'Oréal is an Investor in People, employing 52,000 people in 130 countries. With an annual turnover of £14.5 billion in 2004, 4% of the group's turnover is invested in R&D every year. The company is looking to recruit entrepreneurs with creative flair and drive who can bring their experiences to a dynamic and passionate working environment. International mobility across these functions and brands, and fast progression, are hallmarks of a L'Oréal career.

Each year L'Oréal recruits 30 graduates onto their Graduate Development Programme, into: Commercial, Marketing, Supply Chain & IT and Engineering. The year-long individually tailored programme provides on-the-job placements in different business areas. L'Oréal regards their graduates as future General Managers therefore place a tremendous amount of importance on training.

Internships are also available every year for students and graduates and are often the first step to a career with L'Oréal. They offer the chance to work on live projects. L'Oréal also runs two international competitions for students: 'Brandstorm', L'Oréal's international marketing competition for undergraduates, gives teams the opportunity to experience being international Brand Managers. 'The e-Strat Challenge' is an on-line business game for undergraduates and MBA students, offering a chance to step into the shoes of a General Manager and run a cosmetics company. Please visit www.brandstorm.loreal.com and www.e-strat.loreal.com for more details.

To BUILD BEAUTY, WE NEED TALENT.

"BEAUTY IS ENTREPRENEURSHIP. WORKING IN A TEAM OF PASSIONATE AND DYNAMIC INDIVIDUALS BRINGS OUT THE BEST IN ME."

Richard t.

NATIONAL ACCOUNT CONTROLLER, L'ORÉAL UK

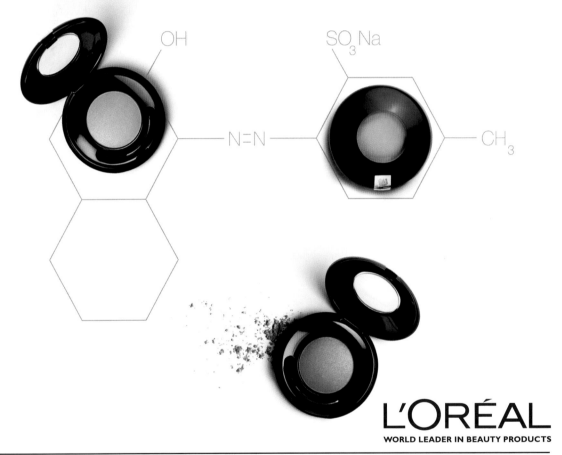

L'ORÉAL
WORLD LEADER IN BEAUTY PRODUCTS

JOIN US. WITH 52,000 EMPLOYEES IN MORE THAN 130 DIFFERENT COUNTRIES, EVERY YEAR L'ORÉAL LAUNCHES 500 NEW PRODUCTS THROUGHOUT THE WORLD.

GRADUATE DEVELOPMENT PROGRAMME. EVERY YEAR L'ORÉAL TAKE ON 30 OF THE MOST TALENTED GRADUATES FROM A WIDE RANGE OF UNIVERSITY COURSES, NATIONALITIES AND BACKGROUNDS INTO COMMERCIAL, MARKETING, SUPPLY CHAIN AND ENGINEERING OPPORTUNITIES. WE OFFER GRADUATES A TAILOR-MADE DEVELOPMENT PROGRAMME WHICH INVOLVES THREE ON THE JOB PLACEMENTS SUPPORTED BY STRUCTURED LEARNING. ENJOY RESPONSIBILITY FROM DAY ONE, THE SUPPORT OF A MENTOR AND A PERSONALISED FAST-TRACK CAREER WITH INTERNATIONAL OPPORTUNITIES. LIKE YOU, WE ARE RESULTS FOCUSED AND LOOK FOR TRUE ENTREPRENEURS WITH CREATIVE FLAIR AND DRIVE WHO CAN BRING THEIR REAL LIFE EXPERIENCES TO A DYNAMIC AND PASSIONATE WORKING ENVIRONMENT. PLEASE VISIT OUR WEBSITE FOR MORE INFORMATION ON THIS PROGRAMME, INTERNSHIPS AND OUR BUSINESS GAMES: **WWW.LOREAL.CO.UK**

L'ORÉAL PROFESSIONNEL PARIS   REDKEN 5TH AVENUE NYC   MATRIX   KÉRASTASE PARIS   L'ORÉAL PARIS   GARNIER   MAYBELLINE NEW YORK   SOFTSHEEN·CARSON

Linklaters

www.linklaters.com/careers/ukgrads

Vacancies for around
130 **graduates in 2007**
For training contracts starting in
September 2009/March 2010

■ Law

Starting salary for 2007
£31,300

**Universities Linklaters
plans to visit in 2006-7**
Please check with your university
careers service for details of events.

Application deadline
See website for full details.

Contact Details
 graduate.recruitment@
linklaters.com
Turn to page 200 now to request
more information about Linklaters.

Linklaters is the global law firm that advises the world's leading companies, financial institutions and governments on their most challenging transactions and assignments. This is an ambitious and innovative firm: the drive to create something new in professional services also shapes a very special offer to graduates.

The firm recruits graduates from both law and non-law disciplines. Non-law graduates spend a conversion year at law college taking the Graduate Diploma in Law (GDL). All trainees have to complete the Legal Practice Course (LPC) before starting their training contracts. The firm meets the costs of both the GDL and LPC.

While many law firms have strengths in particular areas, Linklaters is strong across the full range of commercial, corporate and financial law; this makes the firm an especially stimulating place to train as a business lawyer. The training contract is built around four six-month seats or placements in a range of practice areas. This develops well-rounded lawyers, but it also helps trainees plan their careers after qualifying.

Linklaters people come from many different backgrounds and cultures; by working together to achieve great things for clients, they are encouraged to achieve their own ambitions and potential. Training with Linklaters means working alongside some of the world's best lawyers on some of the world's most challenging deals. The firm expects a lot of its trainees, but the rewards – personal and professional as well as financial – are very high indeed.

You don't need a law degree to train as a lawyer.

If you've never studied law, how and why should you become a City lawyer? We think it's one of the most intellectually stimulating and professionally rewarding career choices you can make, but then, we would say that wouldn't we? Maybe people in other professions get just as excited about their thing as we do about ours. All we're saying is, this is one option you shouldn't ignore – even if you've never thought of it before.

So let's get back to basics. We've produced a booklet that explains what business lawyers actually do all day. 'Why be a lawyer' is available at most careers services, and you can also order a copy online. In fact, there are all kinds of things on our website that you might be interested in. We believe you can't make a sensible career choice unless you understand what a job actually involves, so we've tried to convey the Linklaters experience in a number of different ways.

Of course, the gold-standard, bells-and-whistles introduction to working life is the Linklaters vacation scheme, but it does come with a bit of a health warning. People who spend a few weeks with us are very likely to come back and train with us as lawyers. Is it something we put in the tea? Or is this just a great place to build a career? Find out at linklaters.com/careers/ukgrads

Linklaters

What do you need to know?
www.linklaters.com/careers/ukgrads

Meena Oduru has just been offered a training contract.
She describes her experiences of the vacation scheme process on our website.

You first  Lloyds TSB

Vacancies for around 100 graduates in 2007

- Accountancy
- Finance
- General Management
- IT
- Retailing

Starting salary for 2007
£25,000-£28,450
Plus sign-on bonus of £5,000.

Universities Lloyds TSB plans to visit in 2006-7
Birmingham, Cambridge, Cardiff, Durham, Edinburgh, Leeds, Manchester, Nottingham, Sheffield, Warwick
Please check with your university careers service for details of events.

Application deadline
31st January 2007

Contact Details
✉ graduates@lloydstsb.co.uk
Turn to page 200 now to request more information about Lloyds TSB.

The Lloyds TSB Group is one of the UK's leading financial services organisations. Offering a range of products as diverse as personal and corporate banking, mortgages, insurance, investments and pensions, the Lloyds TSB, Scottish Widows and Cheltenham & Gloucester brands are recognised and trusted by millions.

Lloyds TSB's business reaches much further than the High Street. In fact, they employ almost 80,000 people across 20 countries worldwide. Unsurprisingly, the opportunities for graduates are just as diverse. They look for graduates with the ambition and potential to lead the business as a whole. Graduates can join the Group Leadership Programme, Group IT Leadership Programme or on a specialist programme in Finance, linked to the CIMA qualification. Whichever route graduates choose, the training will be tailored to accelerate potential. Lloyds TSB even have their own award-winning corporate university – one of the largest in Europe.

Lloyds TSB will develop leadership potential in a demanding environment – combining formal business-related courses with a series of placements to help graduates become fully-qualified professionals.

A graduate's development will be supported by an experienced Graduate Trainee, a Senior Manager and a Graduate Development Manager. Lloyds TSB will also provide full financial support for relevant professional qualifications.

Lloyds TSB is looking for high academic achievers with energy, initiative and exceptional interpersonal, and problem-solving skills. In return, they will offer successful applicants an excellent salary, flexible rewards, banking benefits, share options and most importantly, an enjoyable work-life balance.

You first  Lloyds TSB

I want to be a

big fish in a

big
pond

You can have it all

www.lloydstsbgraduate.co.uk

Lovells

www.lovells.com/graduates

**Vacancies for around
90 graduates in 2007**
For training contracts starting in 2009

Law

Starting salary for 2007
£31,000

**Universities that Lovells
plans to visit in 2006-7**
Belfast, Birmingham, Bristol,
Cambridge, Dublin, Durham,
Edinburgh, Exeter, Leeds,
Leicester, London,
Manchester, Nottingham,
Oxford, Reading, Sheffield,
St Andrews, Warwick.
Please check with your university
careers service for details of events.

Application deadline
31st July 2007

Contact Details
✉ recruit@lovells.com

Turn to page 200 now to request
more information about Lovells.

Lovells is one of the world's leading international business law firms with 26 offices in the major financial and commercial centres across Europe, Asia and the United States.

The firm's international strength across a wide range of practice areas gives it an exceptional reputation not only for corporate transactional work, but also for other specialist areas including dispute resolution, banking, intellectual property, employment, EU/competition, insurance and commercial.

Lovells clients include some of the world's most prestigious and demanding, high profile businesses. As a consequence of the high profile work the firm does, applicants need to have achieved excellent academic results from GCSE onwards. A 2.1 (or equivalent) is the minimum standard of degree applicants should hold or be expecting to achieve. Applicants need to be happy working in a team yet capable of, and used to, independent action. They will need to demonstrate ability and desire for lateral thinking, be capable of close attention to detail, and be ambitious to succeed in a top law firm.

Lovells treats continuous training and development as a priority for those undertaking the LPC, trainees and qualified lawyers. All trainees receive approximately 160 hours of formal training over the two year training contract, including the Professional Skills introductions to the specialist groups at Lovells. Trainees spend six months in four different areas of the practice, and have the option of spending time in their second year of training in an international office or on secondment to the in-house legal department of a major client.

Lovells

REACH
ADDICTIVE
ASTUTE
CONCERT

www.lovells.com/graduates

We are looking for the next generation of Lovells lawyers: academically bright graduates with an aptitude for lateral thinking and exceptional levels of commitment to contribute not only to the firm's future growth and development but their own as well.

We build dynamic working teams and encourage ideas and input from every member. An innovative approach and creative thinking in every area of legal work makes Lovells an exciting and challenging place to work.

The work at Lovells is varied. Our international strength across a wide range of practice areas gives us a reputation not only for corporate transactional work, banking and litigation, but a range of other specialist areas too.

To find out more about training at Lovells visit our graduate website at www.lovells.com/graduates or contact:

Clare Harris or Caroline Lindner
Lovells, Atlantic House,
Holborn Viaduct
London EC1A 2FG

Telephone: +44 (0)20 7296 2000

Alicante
Amsterdam
Beijing
Berlin
Brussels
Budapest
Chicago
Dusseldorf
Frankfurt
Hamburg
Ho Chi Minh City
Hong Kong
London
Madrid
Milan
Moscow
Munich
New York
Paris
Prague
Rome
Shanghai
Singapore
Tokyo
Warsaw
Zagreb

YOUR M&S

www.marksandspencer.com/gradcareers

Vacancies for around
100 **graduates in 2007**

■ **Human Resources**

■ **Retailing**

Starting salary for 2007
£21,000-£24,500

**Universities that
Marks & Spencer
plans to visit in 2006-7**
Aston, Bath, Belfast,
Birmingham, Cambridge,
Cardiff, Dublin, Durham,
Edinburgh, Exeter, Leeds,
London, Manchester,
Nottingham, Sheffield,
Strathclyde, Warwick
Please check with your university
careers service for details of events.

Application deadline
December 2006

Contact Details
Turn to page 200 now to request more
information about Marks & Spencer.

Marks & Spencer. A name that has always been associated with quality. Whether it's their food, clothes and furnishings or the outstanding customer service they provide, they strive to ensure they always offer the very best. And their graduate scheme is no exception.

Graduates will enjoy the kind of thorough grounding in retail that few other organisations can provide. Over the course of around 12 months, they will take on between three or four placements, enjoying a mixture of on-the-job training and classroom tuition.

Most of Marks & Spencer's trainees join them in a store-based role, and are placed on a fast-track route into senior level retail management. If everything goes as planned, within a year they could be running their own small store or managing a whole department of a larger one. M&S are also one of the few retailers to offer a HR programme. By choosing this route, graduates will have the chance to develop specialist skills and expertise, and build a successful, long-term career. And for something outside the store environment, there's always the Head Office. For more information on the opportunities in these areas, please visit their website.

Marks & Spencer look to recruit only the most talented people. People who have the drive and ambition to make the most of all the opportunities they offer. People who can provide the level of service their customers have grown to expect. And people who can match the energy, vision and ideas that have kept them at the forefront of the retail industry.

With just 100 places on offer, how will you improve your chances?

eople will try anything to get on our graduate scheme. Not surprising, considering within 12 months you'll cover very aspect of a successful retail operation and gain the skills and experience you need to become a great anager. So what will give you an advantage when it comes to securing a place?

'ell, we're looking for the future leaders of our company, so the ability to motivate and inspire will be key. Like any anager you'll also need to be able to deliver results. But perhaps most importantly we're after people with new eas, and the drive to implement them, because to build on our success we need to constantly evolve.

urther advice about the qualities you'll need (the ability to pass yourself off as a none too convincing lampshade ot being one of them), can be found at www.marksandspencer.com/gradcareers

he Graduate Scheme everyone wants to get onto.

Marks and Spencer plc is an equal opportunities employer.

Mars

The ultimate business school

www.mars.com/ultimategrads

Vacancies for around
20-30 graduates in 2007

- Engineering
- Finance
- General Management
- Marketing
- Research & Development
- Sales

Enjoy

that

feeling of

inevitable

success.

Starting salary for 2007
£25,500+

**Universities that
Mars Incorporated
plans to visit in 2006-7**

Bath, Birmingham,
Cambridge, Durham,
Edinburgh, Glasgow,
London, Manchester,
Newcastle, Nottingham,
Oxford, St Andrews,
Strathclyde, Warwick, York
Please check with your university
careers service for details of events.

Application deadline
26th January 2007

Contact Details

✉ mars.graduate@eu.effem.co.uk

Turn to page 200 now to request more
information about Mars Incorporated.

Mars, Uncle Ben's, Snickers, Whiskas, M&M's, Dolmio, Twix, Pedigree, Maltesers… these are just some of the household name brands that form the global, $14 billion Mars portfolio. It's little wonder then that it takes 30,000 associates on 140 sites in 60 countries to run a business on this scale. It will also come as no surprise that when recruiting graduates, Mars settles only for the highest calibre.

Surprisingly, Mars Incorporated is still a private, family-owned business. They invest only their own profits in developing the organisation. This means that their graduates – razor sharp business-leaders-in-the-making – get to take more educated risks, explore more avenues and achieve more of everything.

Mars offers development programmes for those who want to specialise in finance, marketing, sales or R&D. These programmes allow graduates to expand their knowledge, stretch their talent and discover a wealth of new skills. Graduates will have access to Mars' tailored training curriculum covering topics such as presentation, leadership and people management skills. Mars supports all its graduates to achieve professional qualifications with financial sponsorship and study leave. Also, the organisation offers a one-year industrial placement for those looking to complement their degree with challenging work experience.

If that wasn't enough, there's the grand prix of graduate schemes – the Mars Management Development Programme. This is a three-year fast-track for the best graduate talent, the opportunity to gain unparalleled experience across all areas of the business, and a platform for a career with no limits.

Mars

The ultimate business school

Stay

You've already proved yourself at university – whether you've finished it yet or not. Now it's time to turn academic excellence few can match into career success that few will emulate. Visit www.mars.com/ultimategrads

a cut

above.

i'm lovin' it

Vacancies for around
150 **graduates in 2007**

■ General Management
■ Retailing

Starting salary for 2007
£18,500-£21,500

Universities McDonald's plans to visit in 2006-7
Please check with your university careers service for details of events.

Application deadline
Year-round recruitment

Contact Details
✉ managementrecruitment @uk.mcd.com
☎ 020 8700 7007

Turn to page 200 now to request more information about McDonald's.

Forget the myth that says McDonald's only offers McJobs. The reality is very different – and far more interesting. McDonald's management careers offer exceptional challenge and support, some excellent rewards and all the potential of a world-famous brand.

Their 20-week management development programme prepares graduates for running a restaurant – Business Management as they call it. This is commercial management in its fullest sense. Graduates gain valuable operational experience in the restaurants, and, as importantly, benefit from wide-ranging commercial exposure. They cover everything from leadership and people development to cash control and profit maximisation.

Provided they excel on the programme, within a few years of joining, graduates could be managing a £million business with a 60-strong team: a McDonald's restaurant. After that they join a management career path that could lead right up to Executive team level. Naturally, not everyone will climb that high. But as long as they have leadership potential and can make the most of the award-winning training, there's no reason why graduates shouldn't set their sights high.

McDonald's urges graduates to do some soul-searching before applying. McDonald's managers set the tone of their restaurants, bringing the best out of their team. To build their businesses, they have to display energy, commitment and hard work every day. And they need to combine both decisiveness and sensitivity; ideas and action. Only by blending all these qualities will graduates excel on one of the most stimulating management development programmes around.

McPackage
£45,000pa

Not bad for a McJob

Less than three years after joining as a **Trainee Business Manager**, you could be running your own restaurant as a Business Manager. As such, you'll shape every aspect of the operation, inspiring your team, boosting sales and marketing, controlling finances and forging all-important community links. In short, you'll answer for the restaurant's performance – and pick up the rewards for its success. Make the business all it could be and you can look forward to a salary and package of some £45,000, which will include some great benefits, not least the chance to take a Mini Cooper as a company car. Apply online at **www.mcdonalds.co.uk/careers** or call our **Recruitment Hotline on 020 8700 7007.**

McKinsey&Company

www.mckinsey.com

McKinsey & Company is a place where recent graduates can have immediate and direct contact with some of the world's top CEOs and public leaders and where their opinions are encouraged and valued.

As a leading global management consultancy, McKinsey's goal is to provide distinctive and long-lasting performance improvements to their clients, who range from governments and multinationals to charities and entrepreneurial firms.

As business analysts, graduates work as part of a small team comprising of client and McKinsey colleagues from around the world. Dedicated to one project at a time, they contribute fully: gathering and analysing data, interviewing, coaching and listening, making recommendations and presenting these findings to clients. McKinsey's work cuts across every business sector; from multimedia to energy, banking to retail, and e-commerce to healthcare.

McKinsey provides invaluable skills, hands-on experience and a thorough grounding in the commercial world. Business analysts are supported with day to day mentoring and coaching, coupled with comprehensive formal training programmes from day one, in order to develop their full potential. McKinsey's commitment to development begins prior to joining with funding for overseas language tuition and training in business basics.

McKinsey believes that bright, highly motivated newcomers to the business world can bring fresh and innovative insights to bear on their clients' problems. Each year, McKinsey hires a number of outstanding graduates and Masters students from a diverse range of academic disciplines as business analysts.

greater
expectations

We welcome applications from all degree
disciplines. To find out more please visit
www.mckinsey.com

McKinsey&Company

MERCER
Human Resource Consulting

Vacancies for around
80 graduates in 2007

- Consulting
- Finance

Starting salary for 2007
Up to £27,000

Universities that
Mercer HR Consulting
plans to visit in 2006-7
Birmingham, Bristol,
Cambridge, Durham,
Edinburgh, Glasgow, Leeds,
Liverpool, Manchester,
Newcastle, Nottingham,
Oxford, Sheffield,
St Andrews, Warwick
Please check with your university
careers service for details of events.

Application deadline
Year-round recruitment

Contact Details
✉ graduates@mercer.com
Turn to page 200 now to request
more information about Mercer
HR Consulting

Mercer Human Resource Consulting Limited is one of the world's leading consulting organisations, with over 15,000 employees spread across more than 40 countries. Specialising in all aspects of strategic and operational HR Consulting, they advise some of the biggest multinationals – including 70% of the FTSE 100 and many of the Global Fortune 500.

This is not a career in mainstream HR: graduate roles focus firmly on pension and investment services. It's intellectually stimulating work that challenges technically, and helps graduates shine not just on a local, but a global stage.

In Mercer's Retirement Business, graduates join as Actuarial Trainees and support a variety of actuarial and consultancy projects whilst studying for the actuarial qualification. Or, they become Retirement Analysts and support other Mercer businesses with a wide variety of valuation data and liability calculations.

Alternatively, Trainee Pensions Consultants study for the Pensions Management Institute (PMI) qualification on their way to providing specialist advice as fully-fledged Consultants. However, some instead provide investment advice to clients on how best to structure and invest assets as Investment Consultants. Here, they study for the Investment Management Certificate (IMC), and either the Actuarial or Chartered Financial Analyst (CFA) professional qualification.

Candidates need at least 300 UCAS points and an expected 2:1 honours degree or better (2:2 for the Retirement Analysts role) in a numerate, semi-numerate or business discipline. Actuarial Trainees must also have 'A' level Mathematics at grade B or above. Equivalent qualifications will be accepted.

MERCER
Human Resource Consulting

You'll work with the finest minds in the business.

And be one of them.

Actuaries • Analysts • Consultants

It's one thing to work alongside the finest talent as a graduate, quite another to be considered an equal by the leading lights of our industry. This will give you the confidence to not just develop yourself, but to also improve us – an international and leading HR and related financial advice consultancy – while making the most of a myriad of big-business opportunities.

That could mean anything from making better use of a huge multinational company's pension fund, to creating better, more valuable bespoke benefits packages for their employees. But whatever dynamic range of products you're developing, we can guarantee you a breathtaking list of clients – after all, Mercer advises over 70% of the FTSE 100.

You'll also meet like-minded colleagues wherever you join us, and the high-calibre skills you've already honed will be crucial. With 300 UCAS points (or equivalent) and a minimum 2:1 numerical, semi-numerical or business degree (2:2 for Retirement Analysts), you'll not only thrive in your role, but also enjoy intensive induction courses and supported professional training. To apply, please visit **www.mercerhr.com/ukgrads** or contact our Graduate Team on 0845 600 2389 for more information.

A lot to think about.

Mercer aims to attract and retain the best people regardless of their gender, marital status, ethnic origin, nationality, age, background, disability, sexual orientation or beliefs. All recruitment decisions are made on the basis of relevant qualifications, skills, knowledge and experience for the role.

INVESTOR IN PEOPLE

www.mercerhr.com/ukgrads

MMC Marsh & McLennan Companies

Merrill Lynch

www.ml.com/careers/europe

Vacancies for around
120 graduates in 2007

- Finance
- Investment Banking
- IT
- Research & Development

Vacancies also available in Europe.

Starting salary for 2007
£Competitive

Universities Merrill Lynch plans to visit in 2006-7
Bristol, Cambridge, Durham, London, Manchester, Nottingham, Oxford, Southampton, Surrey, Warwick
Please check with your university careers service for details of events.

Application deadline
See website for full details.

Contact Details
✉ graduate_recruitment@ml.com

Turn to page 200 now to request more information about Merrill Lynch.

Merrill Lynch is one of the world's leading wealth management, capital markets and advisory companies, with offices on six continents. Its wealth of diverse locations, products and services, offers unparalleled opportunities to explore a variety of career options.

As a vital part of Merrill Lynch's ever-growing organisation, new employees will benefit from world-class training programmes. Industry-leading professionals will also help new graduates deliver essential solutions and exceptional results for their clients.

Joining one of the key business areas of Global Markets, Investment Banking, Research or Technology, graduates begin in New York as part of Merrill Lynch's intensive introductory programme. On return to the local office, graduates will be provided with a thorough grounding in all the fundamental tools, techniques and work practices allowing them to succeed in the fast-moving, client-driven environment.

As a penultimate year student, interns are in a unique position to gain an invaluable insight into Merrill Lynch with the ten-week summer programme. With exposure to the business and training from industry experts, the interns' ability to prove themselves could lead to a full-time job offer.

Merrill Lynch welcomes ambitious, confident and highly motivated, individuals with a natural ability to work as part of a team, along with a desire for a future in financial services. Whatever their academic background, they will have an inquiring mind with the ability to communicate complex messages in a clear, simple way. Relevant work experience and foreign languages are an advantage. To apply, visit www.ml.com/careers/europe.

METROPOLITAN POLICE

Working together for a safer London

Vacancies for around TBC graduates in 2007

■ Other

Starting salary for 2007
£29,103
For Police Officers.

Universities that MPS plans to visit in 2006-7
Please visit the MPS website and check with your university careers service for details of events.

Application deadline
See website for full details.

Contact Details
☎ 0845 727 2212

Turn to page 200 now to request more information about the MPS.

One of the world's best known and most respected police services, the Metropolitan Police Service (MPS) aims to make London a safer place for the millions of people who live and work in the capital, and the millions more who visit every year.

The MPS is committed to creating a Police Service that fully reflects the ethnic and cultural profile of the population. That's why it's essential that graduates have genuine respect for diversity together with the sensitivity to work effectively with London's many different communities.

A career with the MPS gives the opportunity to enjoy a uniquely challenging and rewarding role with variety and the potential for development.

As a Police Officer, the MPS offers an excellent financial package and development prospects to rival the private sector. In addition, it is also one of the most personally rewarding vocations available.

Graduates with confidence in their leadership abilities, can apply to join the Police Officer High Potential Development scheme (HPD). Leadership ability is the key quality and the scheme is designed to identify and enhance management and command skills through tailored training. The HPD scheme provides a structured route to some of the most senior positions in the MPS.

Alternatively, if the role of police officer is not suitable, graduates can consider a career as a member of Police Staff in areas such as marketing, HR, forensic science, legal services, IT and finance – the list is endless.

Visit the MPS website for more information.

WILL YOUR DEGREE MAKE THINGS BETTER?

You can't use your degree certificate as a tissue to wipe away the tears. Neither can you use it as a sticking plaster to patch up the past. But it can still make seven million Londoners feel safe.

We won't treat you any differently just because you're a graduate. Instead, we'll take what you've learnt, move it out of the examination hall and apply it to the real world. Then it's up to you.

Discover what your qualifications really qualify you for. Seven million Londoners are depending on it.

www.metpolicecareers.co.uk

METROPOLITAN POLICE   Working together for a safer London

me+
GRADUATES

Microsoft®

www.microsoft.com/uk/graduates

Vacancies for around 35 graduates in 2007

- Consulting
- IT
- Marketing
- Research & Development
- Sales

Starting salary for 2007
£23,500
Plus a sign-on bonus.

Universities that Microsoft plans to visit in 2006-7
Aston, Birmingham, Brunel, Cambridge, Kent, London, Loughborough, Manchester, Nottingham Trent, Reading, Sheffield, Warwick
Please check with your university careers service for details of events.

Application deadline
11th January 2007

Contact Details
Turn to page 200 now to request more information about Microsoft.

Microsoft have created an environment where people can do their best. Hard work is expected, but their graduates and students are free to satisfy their intellectual curiosity. Microsoft is somewhere people can think along new lines, explore truly exciting technologies and actually enjoy spending time.

The people who flourish at Microsoft are natural communicators with inquisitive natures, a passion for technology and an instinctive understanding of customers. But what really sets them apart is a drive that raises them above the average whether they join commercial or technical business groups.

The 'Microsoft Academies for University Hires' provide the perfect transition between academic and professional life. Although challenging, they equip graduates with the professional skills and know-how required for a rewarding and successful career at Microsoft. Graduates will tackle unchartered territory, whether working in technical, sales or marketing. It might mean discovering how others work or thinking along new lines. Either way, successful applicants will be stepping outside their comfort zone.

The graduate programme includes residential courses at international locations and self-directed learning. Graduates will be given real responsibility, whilst also having the support of managers and mentors throughout. The basic requirements are a 2:1, creativity, vision, people skills, an inquiring mind and a willingness to learn.

The emphasis during student placements in Reading or London is on supplementing theory learnt at university with real, practical experience. The 48-week scheme starts in July with a week-long induction. Training can include residential courses and self-directed learning.

Curiosity is only natural.

And at Microsoft it's positively life (and career) enhancing. Our company relies on questioning, investigating and generally being nosy in order to advance. As a graduate you'll have to tackle uncharted territory throughout your career, whether you're working in **Technical**, **Sales** or **Marketing**, or on a **student placement**.

To find out more pick up our brochure from your careers service or visit **www.microsoft.com/uk/graduates**

Satisfy your curiosity

Microsoft®
Your potential. Our passion.™

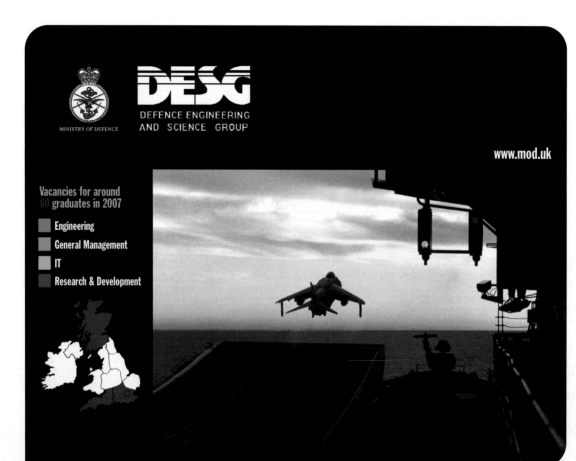

DESG
DEFENCE ENGINEERING AND SCIENCE GROUP

MINISTRY OF DEFENCE

www.mod.uk

Vacancies for around 80 graduates in 2007

- Engineering
- General Management
- IT
- Research & Development

Starting salary in 2006
£20,293
Review in August 2006.

Universities that the MOD plans to visit in 2006-7
Bristol, Cardiff, Southampton, Glasgow, Leeds, Plymouth, London
Please check with your university careers service for details of events.

Application deadline
See website for full details.

Contact Details
✉ sit-desgmktman@mod.uk

Turn to page 200 now to request more information about the MOD.

The Defence Engineering and Science Group (DESG) is a community of 9,000 professional engineers and scientists working within the Ministry of Defence (MOD) Civil Service to equip and support the UK Armed Forces with state of the art technology.

Their work includes research programme management, engineering project management of equipment worth billions of pounds, construction and estates management or in-service support of vehicles and equipment around the globe.

The MOD requires engineers and scientists who are comfortable in their field but who can also take the lead in any situation, building solid working relationships with others whatever their discipline, background or culture. It needs effective communicators, people with organisational skills, creativity and intellect.

In return, graduates can expect first rate development opportunities within the DESG Graduate Scheme and throughout their careers. The DESG Graduate Scheme has been established for almost 30 years and is accredited by some of the leading UK engineering institutions. Initially, the scheme consists of work placements, both in-house and in-industry, intended to provide the breadth and depth required for a career in Ministry of Defence but also demanding that graduates make a meaningful and positive contribution to the business. Graduates are encouraged and supported to achieve professional registration early in their careers and fill a wide range of roles, both as specialists and, as they progress, as team leaders, managers and policy makers.

MOD Civilians are part of the wider Civil Service and are subject to the legal requirements governing Civil Service recruitment. Posts within the DESG Graduate Scheme are reserved and only open to those with British nationality or dual nationality, one of which must be British.

MINISTRY OF DEFENCE

Who said anything about a job for life?

As an engineer or scientist within our DESG Graduate Scheme you'll benefit from outstanding professional development opportunities and as a MOD Civil Servant you don't have to change employer to change jobs.

If you have the credentials, there are many different career paths and hundreds of different jobs to choose from within our internal recruitment market. To find out more visit **www.desg.mod.uk**

Morgan Stanley

Vacancies for around 200 **graduates in 2007**

- **Finance**
- **Investment Banking**
- **IT**

Starting salary for 2007
£Competitive

Universities that Morgan Stanley plans to visit in 2006-7

Bath, Bristol, Cambridge, Dublin, Durham, Edinburgh, Glasgow, London, Manchester, Nottingham, Oxford, Southampton, St Andrews, Warwick, York
Please check with your university careers service for details of events.

Application deadline
15th November 2006

Contact Details
☎ 020 7425 8000

Turn to page 200 now to request more information about Morgan Stanley.

Morgan Stanley is one of the world's largest diversified financial services companies, with a reputation for excellence in advice and execution on a global scale.

Morgan Stanley serves institutional and individual investors and investment banking clients, including corporations, governments and other entities around the world. Truly global, the Firm is a market leader in Europe and Asia as well as the United States: its 59,000 employees work in 600 offices in 30 countries.

Morgan Stanley provides a wide range of services: underwriting, sales, trading and research for almost every financial instrument, as well as merger and acquisition advice, privatisation and financial restructuring, foreign exchange, commodities, and real estate finance. Morgan Stanley also manages more than $625 billion in assets under management and specialises in serving affluent and high net worth individuals in the United States, Europe and Asia. Their worldwide team of professionals works across geographical and product boundaries to serve their clients as one integrated global securities firm.

Morgan Stanley's reputation rests on the abilities and passion of its people, who share a common set of values that begin with integrity and excellence in all they do. The Firm measures success by the success of its clients and the long-term relationships built on rigorous thinking and unsurpassed access to financial markets. They create innovative solutions that help their clients realise new opportunities and solve complex problems.

Morgan Stanley

Are you Morgan Stanley?

Nationwide

Vacancies for around
25 **graduates in 2007**

- Finance
- Human Resources
- IT
- Retailing

Starting salary for 2007
£Competitive

**Universities Nationwide
plans to visit in 2006-7**
Please check with your university
careers service for details of events.

Application deadline
30th April 2007

Contact Details
✉ graduates@nationwide.co.uk
☎ 01793 654205
Turn to page 200 now to request
more information about Nationwide.

Nationwide is the world's largest and most successful building society. They have no shareholders to satisfy so they can direct all their energies and resources into making their customers better off. They treat them fairly and honestly. They don't have to make money out of them. They simply have to make them better off. It's what makes them different.

Nationwide's two-year course gives successful applicants the choice of a Generalist or Specialist option, both of which are made up of three eight-month placements.

The Generalist Programme gives graduates experience of different areas of the business including a retail-based position, a role that develops their management and people skills, and an area that uses their project management and consultancy skills.

The Specialist Programme offers graduates the choice of Finance & Audit, Channel Support, Retail Branch Network, Risk Management, Technology, Banking, Savings & Mortgages, Telephone Channels, Personnel & Development, Treasury or Commercial placements.

Graduates will spend two of their placements in their chosen area, and the third in another part of the business which could be member-facing or one of the other specialist areas.

Whichever programme is chosen, Nationwide's aim is the same: to get graduates started in a career which they will really enjoy and in an area where they can really give their best and make a difference.

Find out more at www.nationwide.co.uk/graduate.

"I wouldn't recommend Nationwide. They've got their priorities all wrong"

He's right, we have. You see, unlike the banks we put people before profits.

So if you share our values and believe you can make a difference to our business, we'd really like to hear from you.

For more information and to apply, please visit
www.nationwide.co.uk/graduate

proud to be different

NATIONAL GRADUATE
DEVELOPMENT PROGRAMME

ngdp.

FOR LOCAL GOVERNMENT

www.ngdp.co.uk

**Vacancies for around
65 graduates in 2007**

▨ General Management

Starting salary for 2007
£21,588
Plus London weighting.

**Universities that ngdp
plans to visit in 2006-7**
Please check with your university
careers service for details of events.

Application deadline
January 2007
See website for full details.

Contact Details
✉ enquiry@ngdp.co.uk
☎ 0845 222 0250

Turn to page 200 now to request
more information about ngdp.

REAL VALUE

REAL CHANGE

The ngdp is a two-year graduate development programme designed to develop future managers and leaders in local government. It was set up to provide local government with the high calibre managers their communities need, and to give committed graduates the training, qualifications and opportunities to make a real difference.

Local government is the largest employer in the UK, with over two million staff in over 400 local authorities and in excess of 500 different occupational areas. These include some that graduates may expect a local authority or council to provide, for example social workers, and many that graduates may not, for instance business analysts, consultants and solicitors.

Local government is going through many positive changes at present and as a trainee on the ngdp, graduates will be at the forefront of these changes. The programme consists of placements in key areas of local authority service. Every participating authority will offer a unique experience, within set national guidelines, and the work is generally high-level and management orientated.

The placements will offer a range of experiences designed to provide a broad understanding of many aspects of local government, including: strategy, service delivery and support service. National training includes study for the postgraduate diploma in local government management, and residential events designed to develop skills. Peer development is also encouraged. Further training and development will be available through the employing authority.

NATIONAL GRADUATE DEVELOPMENT PROGRAMME
ngdp
FOR LOCAL GOVERNMENT
REAL CONCERNS
Crystal Clear Acrylic Coating
Working for local government isn't about dynamic business deals or long lunches. It's about something far more remarkable: delivering real solutions for real communities with real problems. It could see you tackling anti-social behaviour or racism. Equally, it could be about helping a local authority work more efficiently and effectively. Whatever challenges you face, the issues will be complex, difficult and most of all important.
The **ngdp** is a graduate development programme designed to provide local government with the high calibre managers their communities need, and give committed graduates the training, qualifications and opportunities to make a real difference. Over two years you'll undertake a series of placements, covering front line services, support services and strategy. You'll receive a competitive salary and benefits, and excellent personal and professional development opportunities. Most of all, you'll get the chance to see your ideas have real impact. To find out more, visit **www.ngdp.co.uk** or call **0845 222 0250** for a brochure.
Real life. Real work.
www.ngdp.co.uk

www.bringingleadershiptolife.nhs.uk

**Vacancies for around
220 graduates in 2007**

Finance

General Management

Human Resources

Starting salary for 2007
£20,000
Plus High Cost Living Allowance.

**Universities that the NHS
plans to visit in 2006-7**
Please check with your university
careers service for details of events.

Application deadline
December 2006

Contact Details
bringingleadershiptolife@
capita.co.uk
☎ 0870 169 9731
Turn to page 200 now to request
more information about the NHS.

The NHS faces the challenge of leading and improving complex services that matter to everyone in the UK. Made up of over 800 organisations, the scope of career opportunity is vast. The NHS is continuing to undergo the most innovative and sustained period of development in its history. There has never been a better time for ambitious, talented graduates to join a nationally acclaimed scheme dedicated to realising their potential.

The NHS Graduate Management scheme two-year programme has a combination of core learning and specialised threads that support the attainment of a professional qualification in either human resources, finance or general management. Specialist training is at the heart of the scheme, supporting development of personal qualities and management skills. Trainees from each specialism learn together, building relationships across management functions for the future. Personal development continues in years 3 and 4, ensuring trainees are part of the NHS talent pool.

The development graduates receive is complemented by access to senior managers, the opportunity to shadow chief executives and attend Board meetings – and trainees have their own personal mentor, who will be a senior NHS executive.

The scheme is challenging and the rewards can be huge – rapid progress into senior leadership within a major frontline institution and the opportunity to change people's lives.

For further information on the scheme and to apply, please visit www.bringingleadershiptolife.nhs.uk

You don't have to be a brain surgeon to open minds.

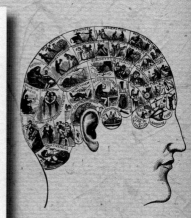

Graduate Scheme
Financial • General • HR

Brain surgeons make a difference to people's lives every day. As an NHS Graduate Trainee you'll also ensure people's lives are improved every day.

We're making a huge investment to transform us into the healthcare service for the 21st century. Now we're looking for the people that will lead it.

Whether your future lies in Finance, HR or General management, our Graduate Scheme offers the chance to gain qualifications while working alongside experienced professionals. It won't be easy. We're looking for people with the passion, drive and determination to make a difference. If you have or are expecting a 2:2 degree in any subject and a hard work ethic that will guarantee results, visit our website to find out more.

www.bringingleadershiptolife.nhs.uk

Oxfam

www.oxfam.org.uk/interns

Vacancies for around
90 graduates in 2007

- Accountancy
- Finance
- General Management
- Human Resources
- IT
- Marketing
- Media
- Research & Development
- Retailing

Starting salary for 2007
£Voluntary

Universities that Oxfam
plans to visit in 2006-7
Please check with your university
careers service for details of events.

Application deadline
Varies by function
See website for full details.

Contact Details
✉ internship@oxfam.org.uk

Turn to page 200 now to request
more information about Oxfam.

Oxfam is a development, relief, and campaigning organisation which is working towards a world without poverty.

Oxfam is about people working together to overcome poverty and suffering around the world. People are Oxfam's greatest resource: over 20,000 volunteers help run Oxfam's famous high street shops; over 600,000 individuals make regular donations; more than a million people worldwide support its campaigns; and countless individuals in more than 70 countries work their own way out of poverty with Oxfam's support.

Oxfam is looking for committed, enthusiastic people to join its voluntary Internship Scheme. For those who are passionate about Oxfam's work and values, and are willing to take responsibility in this high-profile, professional charity, this could be an ideal opportunity. Oxfam interns could be expected to develop campaigns, trial new ideas, work on projects, carry out research, manage an Oxfam shop and more, depending on the internship they apply for.

The Oxfam Internship Scheme is divided into three intakes throughout the year: January to May, June to August and September to December. Although it is unpaid, the scheme provides an allowance for lunch and reasonable travel expenses, and the flexible hours will allow participants to get part-time jobs. Oxfam's Internships are based in shops, regional offices and the Oxford Head Office.

Oxfam is looking for graduates who will inspire others to change the world, because there's no better place to do it!

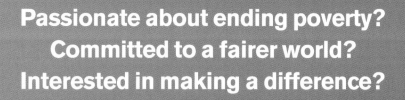

Passionate about ending poverty?
Committed to a fairer world?
Interested in making a difference?

www.oxfam.org.uk/interns

Together we can beat poverty

Oxfam interns clockwise from top centre: Martin, Susanne, Asad, Davide and Stefania

Oxfam GB is a member of Oxfam International. Registered charity no. 202918

COULD YOU?
POLICE

www.policecouldyou.co.uk and www.policehighpotential.org.uk

Vacancies for unlimited **graduates in 2007**

■ **All sectors**

Starting salary for 2007
£20,397

Universities that HPD plans to visit in 2006-7
Birmingham, Durham, Exeter, Leeds, Liverpool, London, Manchester, Newcastle, Northumbria, Oxford, Sheffield, Warwick
Please check with your university careers service for details of events.

Application deadline
Year-round recruitment

Contact Details
☎ 020 7035 50 50
Turn to page 200 now to request more information about HPD.

A career in the police can offer an enticing mix of excitement, challenge and reward. Policing in today's modern police service involves reducing crime and the fear of crime, working in partnership with the public, supporting victims and witnesses and using the latest technology to assist with the detection and prevention of crime.

Careers in the police are not limited to constables working a street beat; there are specialist roles in traffic, fraud, Criminal Investigation Department (CID), Special Branch (combating terrorism), police dog handlers and mounted officers as well as opportunities to move up the career ladder into senior policing positions.

Graduates from any discipline who believe they have leadership potential may be eligible to join the police High Potential Development (HPD) Scheme, once they have secured employment as a police officer in one of England, Northern Ireland or Wales' forces. The scheme provides access to training and career development opportunities including tailored training, challenging promotions aimed at broadening experience of the police service, opportunities to improve leadership and command skills, further education sponsorship and structured support and mentoring.

The HPD scheme assists officers' progression through the ranks. A starting salary of £20,397 on commencing service rises to £22,770 on completion of the initial 16-week training (salaries for the Met Police and City of London Police include a London weighting and London allowance).

I'VE BUILT UP 16 COMPANIES, BUT I COULDN'T REBUILD THE MORALE OF A TEAM OF OFFICERS WORKING ON A CHILD ABUSE CASE.

Stelios Haji-Ioannou
Founder of easyGroup

If you think you could, apply to join the Police and ask about the High Potential Development Scheme. Call 020 7035 5050 or visit our website at policehighpotential.org.uk to find out more.

COULD YOU?

POLICE

The police service is committed to equal opportunities.

PRICEWATERHOUSECOOPERS

www.pwc.com/uk/careers/

Vacancies for around
1200 **graduates in 2007**

- Accountancy
- Consulting
- Finance
- Law

Starting salary for 2007
£Competitive
Plus flexible benefits and an
interest-free loan.

**Universities that
PricewaterhouseCoopers
plans to visit in 2006-7**
Please check with your university
careers service for details of events.

Application deadline
Varies by function
See website for full details.

Contact Details
☎ 0808 100 1500 or
+44 (0)121 265 5852
Turn to page 200 now to request
more information about
PricewaterhouseCoopers.

Graduates will probably have heard of PricewaterhouseCoopers LLP (PwC), but may not know exactly what they do. As a large professional services firm, their work is hugely diverse.

With offices all over the world, they work with an enormous range of clients – businesses, charities and governments – providing services that help to improve the way they work in the short and long-term. From auditing their finances and planning their taxes to identifying the commercial risks they face and assessing the implications of strategic decisions, PwC work in partnership with all their clients creating leading-edge solutions.

All in all, PwC offers graduates a great introduction to the world of business in a supportive and team-oriented environment. And with a range of business groups to choose from, they have something to offer everyone, whatever the subject of their degree and wherever their interests lie. Indeed, they're looking for high-calibre graduates with the thirst and enthusiasm to build a successful career in business.

Graduates will need to be prepared to work hard from day one and in return will benefit from PwC's first-class investment in their people and the continuous professional development that the variety of work can offer. And their supportive culture will give graduates everything they need to excel.

In return for talent and commitment, they pay a competitive salary and have an innovative, flexible benefits scheme.

Across the UK their positions fill up quickly each year so early application is advised. To find out more, visit their website – www.pwc.com/uk/careers/

**Graduate
Opportunities
Nationwide 2007**

**Assurance
Tax
Advisory
Actuarial
Strategy**

We are an equal
opportunities employer.

No ifs. No buts. If you want variety, you should be talking to PricewaterhouseCoopers. Not only are we one of the world's leading professional services firms, we've been voted the UK's Top Graduate Employer in The Times Top 100 Graduate Employers survey for the last three years. We're the one firm for all focused graduates.

www.pwc.com/uk/careers/

P&G

www.pgcareers.com

Vacancies for around
80 graduates in 2007

- Accountancy
- Engineering
- Finance
- General Management
- Human Resources
- IT
- Logistics
- Marketing
- Purchasing
- Research & Development
- Sales

Vacancies also available in Europe.

Starting salary for 2007
£27,000

**Universities that
Procter & Gamble
plans to visit in 2006-7**
Birmingham, Cambridge,
Dublin, Durham, Edinburgh,
Leeds, London, Manchester,
Nottingham, Oxford,
Strathclyde, Warwick
Please check with your university
careers service for details of events.

Application deadline
Year-round recruitment

Contact Details
✉ recunitedkingdm.im@pg.com
☎ 0800 056 5258
Turn to page 200 now to request more
information about Procter & Gamble.

Established almost 170 years ago, P&G is the most admired Fast Moving Consumer Goods company in the world. It has one of the largest and strongest portfolios of trusted, quality brands, including Ariel, Always, Bounty, Braun, Charmin, Crest, Duracell, Gillette, Head&Shoulders, Iams, Lenor, Olay, OralB, Pampers, Pantene and Pringles.

Every day these brands touch the lives of more than two billion people around the world. 140,000 P&G people in 80 countries worldwide work to ensure P&G brands live up to their promise to make everyday life a little better.

P&G attracts and recruits the finest people in the world, because it grows and develops its senior managers within the organisation. This means new starters with P&G can expect a job with responsibility from day one and a career with a variety of challenging roles that develop and broaden their skills, together with the support of training and coaching to help them succeed.

Although best known for marketing and sales, P&G offers exciting careers in all the functions required to operate a major multinational company. These include Customer Business Development (sales & commercial careers), Finance, Human Resources, Information & Decision Solutions (careers adding value to their business processes through IT), Marketing (careers in general management), Product Supply (careers in engineering, manufacturing and supply chain management) and Research & Development. The company looks for talented graduates with broad range of skills demonstrated through their activities and interests. Most functions welcome applicants from any degree discipline.

P&G was voted Fortune Magazine's Most Admired FMCG Company 2006.

Making everyday life
a little better two
billion times
a day…

… now
that's a
new challenge!

A career with Procter & Gamble offers roles with real responsibility from day-one and the training and coaching to help you succeed. With 22 billion dollar brands and operations across 80 countries, you will find your work really does bring a new challenge every day!

Add to this P&G's approach to growing our top leadership within the organisation and you will understand why your continuing development is so important to our success.

If you are ready for this challenge then we are ready for you! Apply online at www.pgcareers.com for vacancies throughout Europe.

Marketing & Sales
Research & Development
Engineering & Manufacturing
Finance
Human Resources
Information Technology

P&G
A New Challenge Everyday

www.PGcareers.com

QinetiQ

www.QinetiQ.com/careers

Vacancies for around
150 **graduates in 2007**

- Engineering
- General Management
- IT
- Research & Development

Starting salary for 2007
£23,000

Universities that QinetiQ plans to visit in 2006-7
Belfast, Birmingham, Bristol, Cambridge, Edinburgh, Glasgow, Leeds, London, Loughborough, Nottingham, Oxford, Sheffield, Southampton, Strathclyde, Surrey, York
Please check with your university careers service for details of events.

Application deadline
Year-round recruitment

Contact Details
Turn to page 200 now to request more information about QinetiQ.

It's time to get inventive

QinetiQ brings the intelligence, imagination and invention of some of the world's leading research scientists to the intractable, insurmountable and frankly implausible. By doing so, they make the impossible an everyday reality.

A world-renowned defence, technology and security company, QinetiQ brings the research rigour and forward thinking required in the defence world to the widest range of civil projects. They offer a similarly broad range of careers covering operational analysis, scientific research, development, test and evaluation and project management – in fields ranging from media to healthcare, aerospace to security and telecoms to transport.

A world leader in the creation and application of technology, QinetiQ's proud heritage includes inventing the jet engine, LCD, flat panel speakers and carbon fibre. So they give their people the freedom, resources and training to push the boundaries of existing knowledge and inspire one another.

QinetiQ seeks around 150 extraordinary new people a year. They look for proactive, analytical, forward-thinking graduates from most science, engineering, IT and numerate disciplines. They offer a good salary and benefits package combined with real quality of life. They also offer a core graduate development programme, the chance to work alongside leading scientists and on-going professional development. So whatever route a graduate takes, they will be surrounded by opportunities.

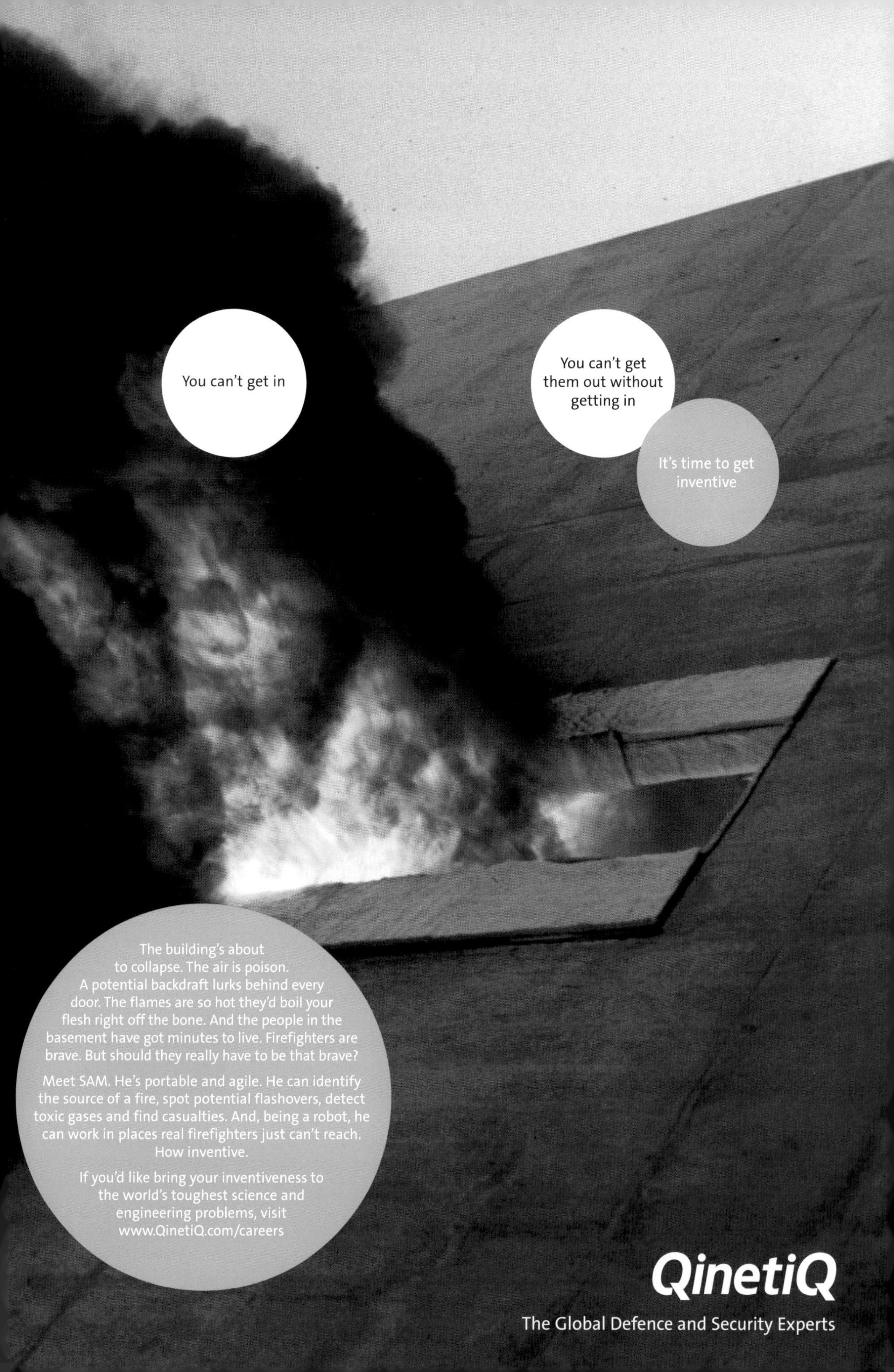
You can't get in
You can't get them out without getting in
It's time to get inventive
The building's about to collapse. The air is poison. A potential backdraft lurks behind every door. The flames are so hot they'd boil your flesh right off the bone. And the people in the basement have got minutes to live. Firefighters are brave. But should they really have to be that brave?
Meet SAM. He's portable and agile. He can identify the source of a fire, spot potential flashovers, detect toxic gases and find casualties. And, being a robot, he can work in places real firefighters just can't reach. How inventive.
If you'd like bring your inventiveness to the world's toughest science and engineering problems, visit www.QinetiQ.com/careers
QinetiQ
The Global Defence and Security Experts

REUTERS

www.reuters.com/careers/graduate

Vacancies for around
40 graduates in 2007

- Accountancy
- Finance
- IT
- Media

Starting salary for 2007
£25,000 - £27,500
Depending on scheme.

Universities that Reuters
plans to visit in 2006-7
Cambridge, Cardiff, Dublin,
Glasgow, Oxford,
Strathclyde, Warwick
Please check with your university
careers service for details of events.

Application deadline
31st December 2006

Contact Details
✉ graduate.recruitment
@reuters.com
Turn to page 200 now to request
more information about Reuters.

Reuters have been providing indispensable news and financial information for over 150 years. Their competitive, fascinating market means they can offer both challenge and variety to graduates who seek these qualities. At Reuters, graduates get to advance their career whilst doing work that is truly meaningful.

Reuters look for a consistently strong academic track record and at least a 2:1 degree or international equivalent. They also prize evidence of mental agility, initiative, tenacity and a flair for innovation. Web literacy and a healthy interest in the financial markets are essential. They offer four graduate programmes, in technology, finance, journalism and business.

Through assignments in different parts of the organisation, these programmes expose graduates to as much of their multi-faceted business as possible. Within their first 12-18 months, it is likely that they will get direct experience of their business by working on an international project.

For individuals with drive and ambition, Reuters graduate programmes provide a platform for creative ideas and limitless scope to make a real impact. They encourage and expect graduates to play a decisive role in defining their own future.

To find out more about the programmes and challenges Reuters offers, read graduate profiles, and apply, please visit www.reuters.com/careers/graduate

Enlighten the world.
Enrich your career.

Be part of the Reuters team.

Is it possible to advance your career while doing something truly meaningful? It is at Reuters. We've been providing indispensible news and financial information for 150 years. And as we look to the future, there are opportunities for talented individuals to join us.

Reuters offers a variety of careers, with competitive compensation packages and advancement potential both locally and globally.

Ready to do something meaningful with your career? Visit **reuters.com/careers/graduate** for more information.

Louise Buckley
Head of Marketing Communications, Business Divisions.
Joined graduate programme August 1999

Edward White
Technology Graduate Trainee. Joined graduate programme September 2005

Rolls-Royce

www.rolls-royce.com/university

Vacancies for around
130 **graduates in 2007**

- Engineering
- Finance
- Human Resources
- Logistics
- Purchasing
- Sales

Starting salary for 2007
£24,000+

Universities Rolls-Royce plans to visit in 2006-7
Bath, Birmingham, Cambridge, Cardiff, Durham, London, Loughborough, Manchester, Nottingham, Oxford, Sheffield, Southampton, Strathclyde, Warwick
Please check with your university careers service for details of events.

Application deadline
Year-round recruitment

Contact Details
✉ peoplelink@rolls-royce.com

Turn to page 200 now to request more information about Rolls-Royce.

Graduates know Rolls-Royce as a company with a great heritage and a bright future – as a high technology engineering company that's a market leader in power generation. But there's more to Rolls-Royce than people think.

They provide gas turbine power for customers all over the world. With 35,000 employees worldwide, they have main sites in the UK, North America, Germany and the Nordic countries. They work on some of the most exciting projects around including participating in the world's two largest combat projects – the Eurofighter and the Joint Strike Fighter – while developing new marine technology that could change ship propulsion forever.

Rolls-Royce require the best supply chain, the strongest finance operation, the most creative deal-makers, the greatest customer focus and the finest engineers to help take them into the future. They have two main programmes especially for graduates. One is the well-established Professional Excellence Programme, a 12-18 month programme designed to develop a high level of competence in a particular career area. The other is the recent Leadership Development Programme (18-24 months), which focuses more on developing leadership skills.

The programmes are tailored to meet the individual needs of the graduate. Whether they're an engineer, an accountant or a purchaser, they'll work with an Early Career Development Advisor to design the blend of job experience, training, project work and other activities that will help them perform to their full potential.

"Today I kept one million passengers in the air." What will you do tomorrow?

Graduate Opportunities

Our graduates are proud to work for us. Involved in exciting, innovative projects such as real time data transfer from engines on the wing, keeping one million people travelling in the air every day courtesy of Rolls-Royce, it's not hard to see why.

As an icon of a century of thought and innovation across the civil and defence aerospace, marine and energy sectors, we offer a wealth of opportunities through two graduate programmes designed specifically to develop your professional or leadership skills to the full. What will you do tomorrow?

To find out more about the opportunities on offer, just visit www.rolls-royce.com/university

Trusted to deliver excellence

www.rolls-royce.com/university

Vacancies for around 300 graduates in 2007

- Accountancy
- Consulting
- Finance
- Human Resources
- Investment Banking
- IT
- Marketing
- Retailing
- Sales

Vacancies also available in Europe, Asia and elsewhere in the world.

Starting salary for 2007
£Competitive

Universities that The Royal Bank of Scotland Group plans to visit in 2006-7

Bath, Belfast, Bristol, Dublin, Durham, Edinburgh, Glasgow, Leeds, London, Manchester, Nottingham, Sheffield, St Andrews, Strathclyde, Warwick
Please check with your university careers service for details of events.

Application deadline
Varies by function
See website for full details.

Contact Details
✉ rbsgrads@tmp.com

Turn to page 200 now to request more information about The Royal Bank of Scotland Group.

The Royal Bank of Scotland Group doesn't stand still. They entered US banking with the acquisition of Citizens Bank and are now a top-ten US commercial banking business. They completed the biggest takeover in British banking history and now have the largest retail network in the UK.

Their partnership with the Bank of China has positioned them as a major player in the world's fastest growing economy. With brands including NatWest, Churchill, Direct Line and Coutts, they are making it happen for more than 30 million customers and 137,000 staff worldwide.

They have over 300 graduate opportunities, ranging from retail banking, marketing, HR and IT to wealth management, insurance and financial markets. They also run a number of placements, to give students a real taste of life at one of the world's largest financial services groups.

As one might expect from a group their size, graduates will be supported via a network of buddies and mentors as well as formal and on-the-job training. They will also have the opportunity to continue studying for professional qualifications or take part in many of their group-funded community programmes to develop skills such as leadership, communication and team working.

Whichever programme is decided upon, graduates can be sure of real responsibility and continued development from day one. In return, they will need at least a 2:1 in any discipline – combined with the focus and tenacity to deliver in a truly international organisation.

MAKE IT HAPPEN

for a business with more people in the States than in Scotland.

The Royal Bank of Scotland Group brings together more than 40 of the world's leading brands and more than 137,000 people. We are a major player in international finance; but we don't tend to shout about it. Instead we focus on getting things done. From acquisitions to organic growth, from Citizens Bank in North America to our partnership with the Bank of China, we make things happen with speed, insight and expertise. Period.

www.rbs.com/graduates

Make it happen

Sainsbury's

www.sainsburys.co.uk/graduates

**Vacancies for around
70 graduates in 2007**

- Finance
- Human Resources
- IT
- Logistics
- Marketing
- Purchasing
- Research & Development

Starting salary for 2007
£22,000

**Universities Sainsbury's
plans to visit in 2006-7**
Aston, Bath, Belfast,
Birmingham, Bristol, Cardiff,
Essex, Lancaster, Leeds,
Liverpool, London,
Loughborough, Manchester,
Newcastle, Nottingham,
Nottingham Trent, Reading,
Sheffield, Strathclyde,
Surrey
Please check with your university
careers service for details of events.

Application deadline
See website for full details.

Contact Details
✉ sainsburys@reed.co.uk
☎ 0845 241 4927
Turn to page 200 now to request
more information about Sainsbury's.

Sainsbury's is a leading FTSE 100 company and a high-profile
name in a fast-moving market. Inspired by their 'Making
Sainsbury's Great Again' review and the 'Try Something New
Today' campaign, the company has enjoyed a year of solid
recovery. Profits are up more than 12%, sales more than 5%.

Customers are experiencing significant improvement. Price, product range,
quality and service have been subject to reviews: the 16 million customers
who now shop at Sainsbury's on a weekly basis are testament to their
success. To build on this success Sainsbury's needs a diverse group of
exceptional graduates, able to bring fresh commitment, talent and ideas:
sharp, smart people, who love the buzz of retail and get a kick from
knowing the inside story.

Graduates will develop leadership qualities, gain business skills, and increase
their capabilities through training. Real business issues dominate, so there's
an enormous amount of responsibility, and the chance to make a real
difference. There are nine schemes: finance, supply chain, customer and
marketing, human resources, buying, product development, IT, property and
product technology. Graduates will have to decide which is right for them.

An essential element of every scheme is a six-month store placement. Only by
exposure to the hectic retail environment will graduates understand the real
significance of their actions elsewhere.

Find out about what makes a business like Sainsbury's tick at
www.sainsburys.co.uk/graduates and decide whether you have the drive,
character and passion for retail that's needed to make it great again.

To most people a Lychee is a strange fruit of little consequence. To a Sainsbury's graduate it means much more. In the past we've struggled to get enough of them on our shelves to meet demand. Now, following our drive to improve the availability of products and the combined efforts of graduates right across the business, any customer with a craving for Lychees will almost certainly be satisfied.

To know the whole story and learn more about how tiny things can make a huge difference visit us at www.sainsburys.co.uk/graduates

Sainsbury's

Vacancies for around 150 graduates in 2007

- Engineering
- Finance
- Human Resources
- IT
- Marketing
- Research & Development
- Sales

Starting salary for 2007
£28,500
UK minimum.

Universities that Shell plans to visit in 2006-7

Aberdeen, Bath, Birmingham, Bristol, Cambridge, Dublin, Durham, Edinburgh, Leeds, London, Loughborough, Manchester, Nottingham, Oxford, Sheffield, Southampton, Warwick.
Please check with your university careers service for details of events.

Application deadline
Year-round recruitment

Contact Details
✉ graduates@shell.com
☎ 0845 600 1819
Turn to page 200 now to request more information about Shell.

Pursue it
A more exciting career experience

Achieving more together

Shell is at the heart of the energy and petrochemical business and is one of the world's most successful organisations. They are totally committed to a business strategy that always balances profits with principles. They are also committed to attracting, training, developing and rewarding world class people for this truly world class business.

From the moment graduates join Shell, their development is of prime importance. Learning by doing, supported by their manager, is key – real responsibility and decision-making are part of life at Shell from day one. Career progression depends entirely on individual ability, talent and ambition.

Working for Shell, graduates could potentially move geographically, functionally and between different businesses. Shell have a strong ethic of promotion from within, supported by a global job opportunity intranet site.

Graduates' academic records are one key factor in assessing applications, but Shell also place emphasis on performance during interviews and assessment centres. Shell have identified capacity, achievement and relationships as critical to high performance.

Shell have a number of pre-employment opportunities: the Shell Gourami Business Challenge, for which applications are welcome from students who will be in their final year when Gourami takes place; the Personal Development Award, for which applications are welcome from non-finalists.

Full details on Shell can be found on their website, www.shell.com/careers.

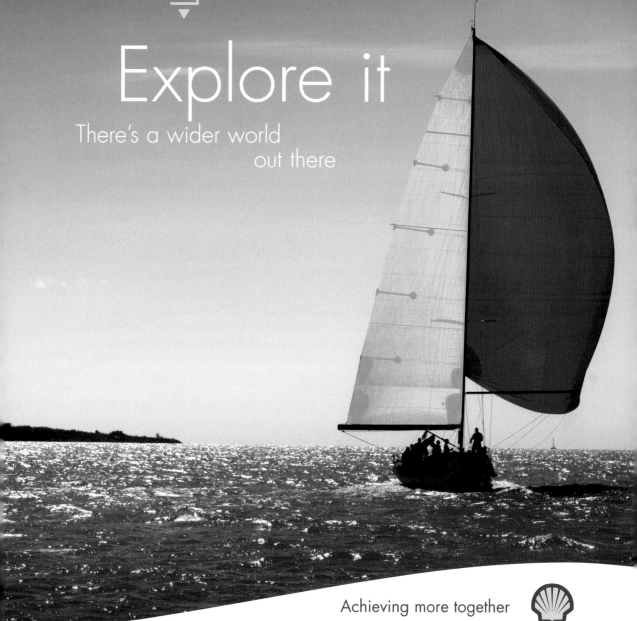

SLAUGHTER AND MAY

Vacancies for around 85-95 graduates in 2007

For training contracts starting in September 2009 and March 2010.

■ Law

Starting salary for 2007
£31,000

Universities that Slaughter and May plans to visit in 2006-7

Please check with your university careers service for details of events.

Application deadline
Year-round recruitment
See website for full details.

Contact Details
✉ grad.recruit@
  slaughterandmay.com
☎ 020 7600 1200

Turn to page 200 now to request more information about Slaughter and May.

Slaughter and May is a leading international law firm whose principal areas of practice are in the fields of corporate, commercial and financing law.

The firm's clients range from the world's leading multinationals to venture capital start-ups. They include public and private companies, governments and non-governmental organisations, commercial and investment banks. The lawyers devise solutions for complex, often transnational, problems and advise some of the world's brightest business minds.

Their overseas offices and close working relationships with leading independent law firms in other jurisdictions mean there are opportunities to work in places such as Auckland, Brussels, Berlin, Copenhagen, Düsseldorf, Frankfurt, Helsinki, Hong Kong, Luxembourg, Madrid, Milan, New York, Oslo, Paris, Prague, Rome, Singapore, Stockholm and Tokyo.

Approximately 85-95 training contracts are available per year for trainee solicitors. Slaughter and May also offers two-week placements during the Christmas, Easter and summer vacations for those considering a career in law.

Following Law School, there is a two year training period during which time trainee solicitors gain experience of a broad cross-section of the firm's practice by taking an active part in the work of four or five groups, sharing an office with a partner or experienced associate. In addition, Slaughter and May offers an extensive training programme of lectures, seminars and courses with discussion groups covering general and specialised legal topics.

Applications from undergraduates of good 2.1 ability from any discipline are considered. Please visit their website for further information.

Your period of training is, of course, very important. But in the context of your career, it's just the beginning. We also put a great deal of emphasis on helping you develop your longer-term career with Slaughter and May – in the practice area you choose.

Look forward in confidence.

SLAUGHTER AND MAY

LEARN MORE *about graduate traineeships and vacation placements at one of the world's most respected law firms by contacting:*

Charlotte Houghton, Slaughter and May, One Bunhill Row, London EC1Y 8YY. Telephone 020 7600 1200.

www.slaughterandmay.com

LEARNING TO LEAD

www.teachfirst.org.uk

Vacancies for around
350 **graduates in 2007**

■ **All Sectors**

Starting salary for 2007
£Competitive

**Universities Teach First
plans to visit in 2006-7**
Bath, Birmingham, Bristol,
Cambridge, Cardiff,
Durham, Edinburgh, Exeter,
Lancaster, Leeds, Leicester,
Liverpool, London,
Loughborough, Manchester,
Newcastle, Nottingham,
Nottingham Trent, Oxford,
Sheffield, Southampton,
St Andrews, Warwick, York
Please check with your university
careers service for details of events.

Application deadline
Final: 30th March 2007
See website for further details.

Contact Details
✉ faq@teachfirst.org.uk
☎ 020 7718 5570
Turn to page 200 now to request
more information about Teach First.

Teach First transforms outstanding graduates into inspiring
leaders, ready to excel in any management career. Combining
intensive teacher training and experience with a unique leadership
and management skills programme, Teach First is a unique
opportunity both to be different and to make a difference.

High-profile recruiters from all sectors recognise that the skills and strategies
developed in teaching are highly relevant and applicable to management
careers. That is why over 80 companies, government agencies and public
bodies are backing Teach First to develop top talent for the future.

Teach First recruits high-calibre graduates from all disciplines to train and
qualify as teachers. At the end of year one, graduates achieve Qualified
Teacher Status, a qualification that means they can return to the teaching
profession at any point in the future. In tandem with their teaching roles,
participants contribute to the extracurricular life of their school and its students,
and participate in courses in strategy, marketing and finance, and skills master
classes. Participants also have the opportunity to attend regular networking
events with industry leaders and benefit from the support of an experienced
network of advisers and coaches.

Joining Teach First means spending two years teaching in a challenging
London, Manchester or Midlands school, preparing and delivering real
lessons to real pupils. It is uniquely demanding but also uniquely rewarding.
Few other career choices offer the same degree of responsibility so early
or the chance to make such an important difference. And after Teach First?
Whether participants choose finance, management, public service or education,
they stand out as exceptional individuals with something special to offer.

Teach First's graduate programme is a unique opportunity to be different and to make a difference. It's an innovative combination of teaching with management skills training and leadership development, plus unparalleled internship, networking and coaching opportunities.

Whatever you aim to do with your career, Teach First.

I taught first

www.teachfirst.org.uk

LEARNING TO LEAD

TESCO

Vacancies for around
150 **graduates in 2007**

- Finance
- General Management
- Human Resources
- IT
- Logistics
- Marketing
- Media
- Purchasing
- Research & Development
- Retailing

Starting salary for 2007
£21,500

**Universities that Tesco
plans to visit in 2006-7**
Aston, Bath, Bradford,
Bristol, Cambridge, Cardiff,
Durham, East Anglia,
London, Loughborough,
Manchester, Nottingham,
Oxford, Southampton,
Warwick
Please check with your university
careers service for details of events.

Application deadline
Varies by function
See website for full details.

Contact Details
✉ graduate.recruitment
@uk.tesco.com
Turn to page 200 now to request
more information about Tesco.

Life at Tesco is incredibly diverse. So the business offers an equally diverse range of graduate opportunities.

Tesco has over 1,900 stores and 250,000 people in the UK, providing everything from iPods and mobiles to clothing, homeware and financial services. What's more, Tesco.com is one of the world's most successful e-commerce operations with over 200,000 orders a week. This variety is reflected in the graduate programmes, with opportunities across the business.

Tesco runs a number of programmes in various areas. In each, graduates will gain first-hand experience of the pace of change in this constantly evolving business. Specialist management programmes offer in-depth knowledge of key functions such as corporate & legal affairs, corporate purchasing, finance, IT, pharmacy, property & engineering, research & analysis, supply chain and Tesco.com. In the general management programmes, graduates can become a manager in areas such as commercial, marketing, personnel or distribution. Or on our Store Management Programme, graduates could be managing up to 800 staff and a £50 million turnover within five years. The Pharmacy Pre-registration Programme provides structured training to help graduates become professional pharmacists.

Tesco look for graduates with strong people, leadership and analytical skills. With, or expecting a 2:1, graduates will be comfortable proposing fresh ideas, and ambitious to move into senior management. In return, Tesco provide all the training, development and hands-on experience successful applicants need to build a rewarding career. This includes annual career planning and a personal development plan throughout their career. Ultimately, though, it is up to graduates to make the most of these opportunities.

The best of everything.
It's not just for our customers.

Graduate opportunities

The Tesco graduate programme. A blend of quality, variety and career nourishment. Because whatever part of our business you join, you'll enjoy responsibility and hands-on commercial experience in, well, bagloads.

To find out more, go to **www.tesco.com/careers**

www.ubs.com/graduates

**Vacancies for around
225 graduates in 2007**

▊ Finance

▊ Human Resources

▊ Investment Banking

▊ IT

▊ Logistics

Vacancies also available in Europe.

Starting salary for 2007
£Competitive

**Universities that UBS
plans to visit in 2006-7**
Please check with your university
careers service for details of events.

Application deadline
10th November 2006

Contact Details
Turn to page 200 now to request
more information about UBS.

UBS, one of the world's leading financial firms, is the largest wealth manager globally, a top tier investment banking and securities firm, a key asset manager and the market leader in Swiss retail and commercial banking.

It's what the employees do that makes UBS a leading global financial services firm. A graduate's skills, ideas and ambition drive the achievement of outstanding results for UBS clients and businesses, in asset management, commercial banking, investment banking and wealth management. 72,000 people in 50 countries share a commitment to excellence. UBS is one firm in many languages.

A graduate's personality and intellect are more important than academic discipline. Best-in-class training and development build the skills and competencies to enable graduates to excel in a chosen role. Ambition and application determine the speed at which graduates progress.

At every stage of a UBS career, top-quality education and development resources support graduates in achieving their goals. UBS's world-class training captures potential and helps graduates hit the ground running.

UBS's global client relationships are built on intimate understanding, so views and opinions are important. As a graduate's insights advance UBS's capability as a world-class enterprise, they contribute toward the decisions that power UBS growth. Above all, UBS wants graduates to be successful. The alignment of career aspirations and business objectives promotes the creation of lasting value for both graduates and UBS.

Your initiative is the engine of our growth. It starts with you.

Do you thrive on challenges? Do you want to collaborate with like-minded co-workers from a range of backgrounds? At UBS, we offer talented individuals a world of opportunities. A diverse culture of mutual respect and support gives all our employees the opportunity to excel. Our world-class training prepares you to be successful. Your skills and ambition are recognized from the moment you join us.

To learn more about life at UBS and apply for a position, go to: **www.ubs.com/graduates**

You & Us

UBS

Wealth | Global Asset | Investment
Management | Management | Bank

Unilever

www.unilever.co.uk/careers

Vacancies for around
50 graduates in 2007

- Engineering
- Finance
- Human Resources
- IT
- Marketing
- Sales

Starting salary for 2007
£26,000

Universities that Unilever
plans to visit in 2006-7
Aston, Bath, Birmingham,
Cambridge, Durham,
Edinburgh, Leeds,
London, Manchester,
Newcastle, Nottingham,
Oxford, Sheffield,
Strathclyde, Warwick.
Please check with your university
careers service for details of events.

Application deadline
15th December 2006
See website for full details.

Contact Details
enquiry@
unilevergraduates.com
☎ 0870 154 3550
Turn to page 200 now to request
more information about Unilever.

> We believe 'dirt is good.'
> Not surprisingly were looking
> for people who aren't afraid
> to get their hands dirty.

Unilever is a leading consumer goods company, making and marketing products in the foods, home and personal care sectors across the world.

In fact over half the families in the world use brands such as Dove, Magnum, Knorr, Persil and Lynx every day. Unilever's mission is to add vitality to life – by helping people feel good, look good and get more out of life. Behind every successful brand lie a number of complex challenges, in all areas of the business: these are what graduates at Unilever will tackle.

Unilever's Graduate Leadership Programme is designed to help graduates reach senior management. Graduates join a specific function in Unilever, where they have a real job with key deliverables and responsibilities from the outset.

Generally, the scheme includes four placements within two years and mobility is essential to get the breadth of experience required. There is excellent training covering leadership development, general business and professional skills. Full support is offered to gain Chartered status or relevant professional qualifications, such as CIPD, CIMA, ImechE, IChemE and IEE.

Unilever wants people with the potential to lead its business. To do this, graduates need to be passionate about business, inspired by profit, competition and customer satisfaction, as well as able to behave with integrity showing both ambition and entrepreneurial spirit.

Unilever's high quality training programmes help graduates develop the expertise and personal qualities they need in order to achieve their career goals. They offer a vast range of opportunities that just have to be taken.

For more information, please visit www.unilever.co.uk/careers

You don't have to turn lead into gold to impress us.
Just toothpaste tubes into tables.

Unilever Graduate Leadership Programme

Visionaries are just as valuable as magicians at Unilever. So if, for example, you could look at the waste from a toothpaste factory in Brazil* and see an opportunity to make chairs, tables, floor tiles and even roofing sheets, you'd fit right in here (*99% of all solid waste generated at the factory is recycled).

That's because creativity is exactly what's made us one of the largest and most successful consumer goods companies in the world. And it's that kind of exciting, out-there, focused kind of thinking that we look for in all of our graduates. Whether you're joining **Marketing, Customer Development, Supply Chain, Information Technology, Human Resources** or **Finance** you'll benefit from a whole range of experiences over up to six placements; you'll enjoy world-beating training; and you'll enjoy all the opportunity you need to become a future leader.

So think: could you solve some of the biggest challenges for brands like Lynx, Dove, Wall's, Flora, Persil and Ben & Jerry's? Could you hold your own with some of the most talented, creative and inspirational people in the industry? If so, we could transform your career. For more information, visit **www.unilever.co.uk/careers**

Could it be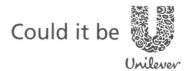

WPP

**Vacancies for around
1-10 graduates in 2007**

- Marketing
- Media

Starting salary for 2007
£22,000-£27,000

**Universities that WPP
plans to visit in 2006-7**
Bristol, Cambridge,
Edinburgh, London,
Nottingham, Oxford
Please check with your university
careers service for details of events.

Application deadline
17th November 2006

Contact Details
✉ hmiller@wpp.com
☎ 020 7408 2204

Turn to page 200 now to request
more information about WPP.

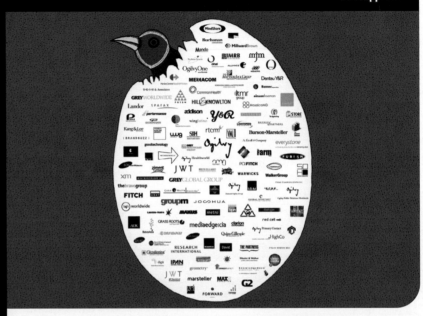

WPP is one of the world's leading communications services groups, made up of leading companies in advertising, media investment management, information, insight & consultancy, public relations & public affairs, branding & identity, healthcare communications, direct, promotion & relationship marketing and specialist communications.

Through its companies, WPP provides communications services to national, multinational and global clients, including many Fortune 500 and FTSE 100 companies. Its 92,000 people work out of 2,000 offices in 106 countries.

WPP Marketing Fellowships, which develop high-calibre management talent with experience across a range of marketing disciplines, will be awarded to applicants who graduate in 2006 or 2007 and have yet to embark on a full time career. Those selected will work in a number of WPP companies and across different marketing disciplines.

WPP is offering several three-year Fellowships, unique multi-disciplinary experience, competitive remuneration and excellent long term career prospects within WPP. It wants people who are committed to marketing, who take a rigorous and creative approach to problem-solving, who are intellectually curious and will function well in a flexible, loosely structured work environment.

The first year of the Fellowship is spent working in a WPP sponsoring company and a personal mentor is assigned to provide overall career guidance. Thereafter, each individual will spend 18 to 24 months working in one or two other WPP companies, with each chosen on the basis of the individual's interests and the Group's needs.

WPP

Marketing Fellowships 2007

Ambidextrous brains required

WPP is one of the world's leading communications services groups. Major brands include JWT, Ogilvy & Mather, Young & Rubicam, Grey Global Group, United, MindShare, Mediaedge:cia, Millward Brown, OgilvyOne, Wunderman, Hill & Knowlton, Burson-Marsteller, Ogilvy Public Relations, Cohn & Wolfe, CommonHealth, Enterprise IG and Landor, among others.

Their specialist skills include Advertising, Media investment management, Information, insight & consultancy, Public relations & public affairs, Branding & identity, Healthcare communications,

Direct, promotion & relationship marketing and Specialist communications: disparate disciplines with two common factors. They are all in business to contribute to the success of their clients. And they all do so through a demanding combination of flair and slog; intuition and logic; left brain and right brain.

WPP will consider applicants who graduate in 2006 or 2007 and have yet to embark on a full-time career. Those selected will work in a number of WPP companies and across different marketing disciplines. Excellent long-term career prospects within a WPP company.

Information leaflets are available from:
Harriet Miller at WPP, 27 Farm Street, London W1J 5RJ
T +44(0)20 7408 2204 F +44(0)20 7493 6819
E-mail: hmiller@wpp.com

Deadline for entry: 17 November 2006
visit our website and apply online at
www.wpp.com

Enter our prize draw to win £5,000 in cash or an iPod Nano!

Make use of our free information service to find out more about the employers featured within this edition of **The Times Top 100 Graduate Employers,** and you could be £5,000 richer when you start your first job!

All you need to do is complete the special *Top 100* **Information Request** card that appears opposite and send it back before the final closing date, **31st March 2007**.

Or you can register your details online at **www.Top100GraduateEmployers.com**

Every completed request card or online registration will be entered into a special prize draw to win the £5,000 in cash.

There are also **50 iPod Nanos** from Apple to be won – one at <u>each</u> of the universities at which the *Top 100* book is distributed, for those who reply by **30th November 2006**.

The information that you request will be despatched to you from the *Top 100* employers directly. This service is entirely free to all UK students and recent graduates.

Fill in the card or go to www.Top100GraduateEmployers.com now!

TOP 100
GRADUATE EMPLOYERS

INFORMATION REQUEST 2006/2007

To request further information about any of the employers featured in The Times Top 100 Graduate Employers and enter our free prize draw to win £5,000, just complete your details and return this postcard.

Your information will be despatched to you directly from the employers, either by email, post or text message via your mobile phone.

NAME _____

UNIVERSITY _____

COURSE _____

TERMTIME ADDRESS

_____

_____

_____

EMAIL _____

MOBILE TEL. NO. _____

Please tick the sectors that you would most like to work in:

ACCOUNTANCY ....☐
CONSULTING ....☐
ENGINEERING ....☐
FINANCE ....☐
GENERAL MANAGEMENT ...☐
HUMAN RESOURCES ....☐
INVESTMENT BANKING .....☐
IT ....☐
LAW ....☐
LOGISTICS ....☐
MANUFACTURING ....☐
MARKETING ....☐
MEDIA ....☐
PURCHASING ....☐
RESEARCH & DEVELOPMENT .☐
RETAILING ....☐
SALES ....☐

☐ PRE-FINAL YEAR   ☐ FINAL YEAR   ☐ I'VE ALREADY GRADUATED

The closing date to request information from these employers and be included in the prize draw to win £5,000 is **Friday 31st March 2007.** If you do **not** wish to be included on our general mailing list and receive information from other relevant graduate employers, please tick here ☐

Please tick the organisations you would like information from:

ACCENTURE ....☐
ADDLESHAW GODDARD .....☐
AIRBUS ....☐
ALDI ....☐
ALLEN & OVERY ....☐
ARCADIA ....☐
ARMY ....☐
ASDA ....☐
ASTRAZENECA ....☐
ATKINS ....☐
BAE SYSTEMS ....☐
BAKER & MCKENZIE ....☐
BARCLAYS BANK ....☐
BARCLAYS CAPITAL ....☐
BBC ....☐
BLOOMBERG ....☐
BP ....☐
BT ....☐
CADBURY SCHWEPPES ......☐
CANCER RESEARCH UK .....☐
CITIGROUP ....☐
CIVIL SERVICE FAST STREAM .☐
CLIFFORD CHANCE ....☐
CORUS ....☐
CREDIT SUISSE ....☐
DATA CONNECTION ....☐
DELOITTE ....☐
DEUTSCHE BANK ....☐
DLA PIPER ....☐
DSTL ....☐
ERNST & YOUNG ....☐
EVERSHEDS ....☐
EXXONMOBIL ....☐
FINANCIAL SERVICES AUTHORITY ....☐
FRESHFIELDS BRUCKHAUS DERINGER ....☐
FUJITSU ....☐
GCHQ ....☐
GLAXOSMITHKLINE ....☐
GOLDMAN SACHS ....☐
GOOGLE ....☐

GRANT THORNTON ....☐
HBOS ....☐
HSBC ....☐
IBM ....☐
JOHN LEWIS ....☐
JPMORGAN ....☐
KPMG ....☐
L'ORÉAL ....☐
LINKLATERS ....☐
LLOYDS TSB ....☐
LOVELLS ....☐
MARKS & SPENCER ....☐
MARS ....☐
McDONALD'S RESTAURANTS ..☐
McKINSEY & COMPANY ......☐
MERCER HR CONSULTING ...☐
MERRILL LYNCH ....☐
METROPOLITAN POLICE .....☐
MICROSOFT ....☐
MINISTRY OF DEFENCE ......☐
MORGAN STANLEY ....☐
NATIONWIDE ....☐
NGDP FOR LOCAL GOVERNMENT ☐
NHS ....☐
OXFAM ....☐
POLICE HPDS ....☐
PRICEWATERHOUSECOOPERS ☐
PROCTER & GAMBLE ....☐
QINETIQ ....☐
REUTERS ....☐
ROLLS-ROYCE ....☐
ROYAL BANK OF SCOTLAND GP ☐
SAINSBURY'S ....☐
SHELL ....☐
SLAUGHTER AND MAY ......☐
TEACH FIRST ....☐
TESCO ....☐
UBS ....☐
UNILEVER ....☐
WPP ....☐

THE INSTITUTE OF CHARTERED ACCOUNTANTS IN ENGLAND & WALES ☐